YOUR LIFE

Why the Silver Lining in Life's Trials Is Actually Gold

Gary Larson

ISBN: 9781611660234

To my wife Joey . . . the most important person in my life.

Acknowledgements

This book would not have been possible without the help of many family members, friends and professionals. I appreciate the teaching moments, the heartfelt direction and the enthusiastic encouragement that you offered me over the last year to make this a reality. Thank you.

Contents

Contents

About the Author

Gary and Joey Larson have spent much of the last twenty years residing in both Florida and Utah. They have four children, a new daughter-in-law (see inset) and their dog Niner. Gary spent most of his adult work life as an entrepreneur engaged in various business activities in tourism, real estate and product development. He received his BS degree at Princeton University and MBA at Brigham Young University. He is an avid journal keeper and enjoys looking for the underlying principles of life found in everyday living.

Foreword by James R. Chambers

My mother told me I'd make great friends in college. Friends that would be with me for the rest of my life. As usual, she was right. One of those friends wrote the book you are about to read.

I met Gary Larson in the fall of 1975, as we were incoming college freshmen, which makes us friends now for over 36 years. He was a natural leader, and coupled with the fact that he looked about as lost as I felt, I was quickly drawn to him. Through his stories I learned about how he grew up in Central Florida, about his high school, his friends and his family. He was a wonderful storyteller—funny, humble, human—and always with a point worth thinking about.

Over the years our lives have taken different paths. We share the fact that we've had long and wonderful marriages, blessed by great families. But our professional paths have been quite different. If I told you *my* story I think you'd fairly easily say, "you've taken the big company executive path." Gary's path is a little harder to characterize. You see, he's done more things than most people even have the courage to think about. Couple that with a rich personal life and deep spirituality and his life's warehouse of storytelling material is overflowing!

When he called me to tell me he was going to write a book . . . well, I wasn't surprised. I assumed it would be another life challenge he'd embrace and one more set of experiences that would make him even more interesting. I didn't know if it would be short or long, fact or fiction . . . but I did know it would be heartfelt and original.

I love stories and I love storytellers . . . even been known to tell a few myself. I love stories that make me think, and stories that make me smile. The stories in this book do that and more. They are lightly written but deeply engaging, and they filled my heart.

This is a beautiful book, humanly told. Sit down with it and read a little or a lot at a time. Jump around. Re-read your favorite sections. But most importantly, translate it into the language of your life and think about what's important to you.

Go ahead and read it, I recommend it highly.

It's from my friend the storyteller . . . God bless him.

HighFive Your Life

Most of the shadows of this life are caused by standing in one's own sunshine.
—Ralph Waldo Emerson

Giving a high five is a universal and well understood symbol of congratulations and celebration. There is no language barrier or cultural interpretation that gets in the way. It just feels good to all those involved.

It would be hard to imagine that anyone reading this book has not given someone a high five sometime in their life. I'm sure that most people have given or seen given multiple high fives. This high energy exchange most likely has its beginning in sporting events where the excitement of the moment cannot be contained. It could be after an incredible run or catch in football, a homerun in baseball, or a last second buzzer beater in basketball. You name the sport and there are high five moments throughout the event.

What is less certain is whether people ever give themselves a high five. When was the last time you actually said to yourself that you did a nice job at something? Are we so self-critical that we do not notice the incredible things that surround us every day? Do we look for the good that can be found amongst all of the bad? Is a high five to be reserved for only those making amazing plays in sports or is watching your kid catch his or her first fish or getting to hug grandma or finding a nugget of wisdom in your life's experiences also deserving of a high five?

My Son Taylor with his Grandpa Robert

A high five is normally a two person exchange. Combine the words "high five" into one word—HighFive—and let that represent a high five given by you to you. HighFive Your Life is a message for all to look for the good in your life and to give yourself a high five because your life is filled with examples where wonderful principles of life are being played out every day. These everyday experiences are determined by decisions you make, by decisions that others make, by not making a decision, by unavoidable circumstances and by avoidable circumstances. They are what you and I go through when we simply journey through life. As you look for and identify these principles you will find that your life is filled with wonderful teaching moments for you and for others. When you do this I think that you will also find that your measure of peace and happiness increases.

This book is not an exhaustive attempt to "teach" you about happiness or to reveal some previously unknown scientific research concerning happiness, but instead, I hope it provides a catalyst for a thought provoking and inspired search for peace and happiness, the possibilities of which are already woven into the fabric of your life. In the brief first section of the book I will share my reasons for writing it. I will explain why I believe so strongly that the worth of a soul is great and why there is hope for you to find peace of mind in this life despite the sometimes very difficult road we travel. I will explain why the stories of your lives are filled with immense wealth if you look for it.

In the second section I will share some of my life's stories. I will use them to share several concepts or principles that have helped me find peace and happiness in this life. I hope that throughout this book you can relate to the stories I share in a way that makes your own life's stories begin to glitter with gold as you find the treasures in the principles of life that are there and that you own. Your life is truly deserving of a high five.

HighFive Your Life

Section One

The Reasons

CHAPTER 1

A Voice of Thunder

Follow the path of the unsafe, independent thinker. Expose your ideas to the dangers of controversy. Speak your mind and fear less the label of 'crackpot' than the stigma of conformity. And on issues that seem important to you, stand up and be counted at any cost.

—*Chauncey Depew*

The clouds outside looked more ominous than the thunderstorms to which I was normally accustomed. That is saying a lot since I grew up in Central Florida, lightning capital of the world. No, these were different. They looked like a mass of dark cotton balls. The front extended in a clean and easily detectable line, with blue sky behind and overhead and dark clouds looming directly in front of us.

I was nervous and had a right to be. We were on a family RV trip somewhere in Montana looking for a campground in which to spend the night and wait out the storm. The impending weather was bad enough but the thought of riding it out in an RV with my wife and our four children was unnerving. We found a campground and checked into our site. We asked when we checked in where we should go in case of a tornado and were told that the safest place was the block restroom in the middle of the complex. That did not offer me much comfort.

You could sense the building storm in all of its various forms as we walked from the site to the small diner at the campground. The sky was darkening, the wind increasing. Once inside the diner, all I could concentrate on was the constant ticker tape message scrolling across the bottom of the TVs warning of possible tornadoes. However, we seemed to be the only ones in the diner that were concerned.

After dinner, we walked out of the diner and were greeted by the sound of a loud siren blaring a warning. I asked someone what it was for and he didn't know. I had never heard a tornado warning before but how could this be anything else? I headed back towards the RV and my wife ran by the laundry to get what she had left to wash during dinner. The storm was getting closer and the intensity of the situation seemed to get stronger every moment.

Before we made it back to the RV, we passed a man who said that he had just heard on the radio that a tornado was supposed to hit in about two minutes, which would be at about 5:02, as I recall. That put more pep in my step. We got to the RV and grabbed a few things, including a camera, (I did not want to miss my $10,000 video of the week shot) and headed to the designated bathrooms.

On the way there, I began to feel some guilt or compassion for the people in the diner that had not had the benefit of hearing what the man with the radio had told me. I told my family that I had to go try and warn them. I hustled back up to the diner and went inside where people were being served, seemingly unaware of the impending destruction heading our way. I went to the cashier located in the back of the store and asked for the manager who soon came. I told him about the radio and the warning and the 5:02 prediction and we both looked up at the clock. It read 5:02! To my surprise, instead of responding in a hurried fashion, shouting for everyone to seek shelter, he basically dismissed me in a thankful way. I walked away and was about to leave when I felt again that I needed to warn the people regardless of the reluctance of the manager to do so. I walked back in and went to the nearest table where there were several people and a waitress and expressed the warning again, and again I got the same response. I left. My memory keeps telling me that I went back in a third time but I cannot be certain. I was just amazed at the lack of concern on their part.

I hurried back to the bathroom and other people arrived to join us as the hail started and the terrible dark clouds and winds engulfed us. We huddled with other people taking in the spectacle and just hoping that a tornado would not actually happen. Had we had a real tornado, our little bathroom would have offered little hope of protection. It was a feeling of vulnerability with my wife and children that I did not like. I had always enjoyed a good storm. In this instance however, we were in real trouble and completely at the mercy of the elements.

After some time, the storm began to dissipate and everyone made their way back to their RVs somewhat relieved. We watched a movie and had a great evening with the kids and retired to bed thankful for our good fortune to have made it out ok. We later learned that a tornado had touched down but had missed our area.

As we hit the road the next day with me at the wheel, I began to reflect again on the previous night's events. I replayed everything in my mind and began to be uncomfortable with my response to what I perceived as a real emergency and why I had let that diner manager get away with dismissing me. I had credible information that I had passed along to both him and the group having dinner. Why had I allowed them to not take me seriously?

By this time in my life, I had been given many opportunities to speak to large gatherings of people, to manage many employees, to address multiple crisis situations. Why had I not jumped on top of one of the tables and shouted tornado!!! Get to cover!!! Hit the deck!!! . . . or something that reflected the potentially dire consequences that awaited us?

As I drove the RV, I quietly contemplated all of it again and again and finally determined that I was not sure enough of my message to break the embarrassment or shyness barrier the previous night. I expressed my warning and when we both looked at the clock and it was already the predicted time and nothing had happened, and the fact that other people there did not seem to be interested, I lost my voice. I was no longer completely sure that a tornado was going to hit us and so backed down and allowed myself to be ignored.

On the other hand, had I actually seen a tornado on the way up to the diner, I am sure that I would have run into the place screaming for people to get down or escape somehow. I would not have even looked for the manager. I would have just started trying to save lives.

I concluded that the one thing that made the difference in my "performance" was entirely my commitment to my message, my belief in what I had to say, my confidence in what I knew to be reality. To the degree that I am uncertain, the surrounding environment—be it people or time or anything else—is in a position to alter my message or my impact. To the degree that I am certain of my message, nothing—not shyness, other people, intimidation, timing; nothing—would be able to get me off message and therefore nothing would degrade my ability to impact a situation. I can have a voice of thunder if I am sure of my message.

If we knew we had only a few minutes of life left and we wanted to communicate to those we were leaving behind some final profound counsel, what would our message be? I am sure that we would express our love. We might tell our loved ones to take care of each other, to forgive each other, to be kind to each other. Perhaps we would express our hopes to be together again one day.

If there were time after that I would want to express with all my heart three very important thoughts which are the reasons for this book. They are three life principles of which I am so sure that I would like to shout with a voice of thunder as loudly as the print on the pages of this book will allow:

1. The worth of your soul is great.
2. The pursuit of happiness, though important, should be accompanied also by a pursuit of peace of mind.
3. The stories of your life are filled with experiences that offer incredible teaching and entertaining moments as you find the embedded life principles. With the right perspective, they can help you continually find the good in life despite the sometimes tough realities of life that you will surely encounter.

When you appreciate these three bedrock principles, you will want to give yourself a high five more often. You will want to HighFive Your Life! When you HighFive Your Life you simply see the silver lining in life's struggles and trials, not because it is so obvious, but because you look for it. I would like for my loved ones to know this as assuredly as I do.

Your soul is of great worth. Peace of mind and happiness are within your reach. The silver lining that is in your life's trials is worth gold. In the next three chapters I will explain in a little more detail why I think these are so important.

HighFive Your Life Principle

When you become sure of your message don't be persuaded by those around you to be quiet. Have a voice of thunder.

CHAPTER 2

The Worth of Your Soul Is Great

I know in my heart that man is good. That what is right will always eventually triumph. And there's purpose and worth to each and every life.
—*Ronald Reagan*

When you contemplate giving your life a high five, or a pat on your own back, much of the conviction to do so will come from your certainty that your life means something or has value, and that you believe that there is a purpose in life greater than what you typically struggle with in your day-to-day activities.

This book is not intended to be a "religious" book, but the fundamental basis for my belief that the worth of a soul is great has come from my belief in a loving God. It does not matter to me the direction you take to get there, whether through faith, simple respect for humanity, or scientific thesis, but once you accept that there is an intrinsically great value to a person's soul, the notion that the "value" of a person is determined by daily circumstances begins to fade away.

As you assimilate this into your thinking, it becomes easier to forgive. It becomes harder to "write somebody off," including yourself. You may value a person for what they "do," but it does not affect the priceless value of their "being."

Perhaps we conclude that our son's football coach is incredible. He pushes and teaches our son to do his best. He does not let him be lazy. He teaches him principles that will be useful in life—to work hard, to go the extra mile, to believe in himself. Some may conclude that this football coach's soul is of great worth.

On the other hand, consider a lazy person who steals and goes to prison. After getting out he steals again and goes back to prison. Some may conclude that his soul is of little worth.

I contend that their value to society is not the same measurement as the worth of their souls. It is clear that the football coach is contributing more to society than the lazy thief and that from society's perspective, he has more "value," but their souls are of equal and great worth. You were born already "being" all that you could be. What has yet to be proven is if you will "do" all that you can do.

With this solid base of self worth, you can do and fail and do and fail again. You can have weaknesses and work to overcome them, perhaps sensing that you are not doing all you would like to do for society and your friends, but never falling to the depths where you actually begin to doubt your self worth. You just get up and keep trying, having a firm foundation and knowledge that your life is special and that your ultimate worth is not affected by your successes and failures in society.

My purpose in this book is not to produce great scientific studies that prove this concept. Think about it. Does it make sense to you? Consider the ramifications. From this base of self worth, you can begin to make your difference in the world. You can work hard for many good causes including yourself. When you do good things you impact society in a good way. You provide value to society and to yourself. You feel better. You can fight to overcome your weaknesses and fight to achieve your goals, but when you fail, which you will often do, you do not fall all the way to the bottom because your self worth is not affected by the events in your life.

You should not interpret the value that society places on you with the worth of your soul. They are two distinct considerations. Though everyone may have a desire to be a "star for a day," you are simply worth more than any value that society could ever place on you. We should do our best to accomplish goals and make positive contributions to those around us, but know this: you are already special in the eyes of a loving God and His love will always provide a base below which your worth will never fall.

HighFive Your Life Principle

Your soul was born with great worth and that worth is not affected by your successes and failures in society.

CHAPTER 3

Peace of Mind—
The Master of Happiness and Sadness

True peace of mind is not dependent on circumstances. It comes from the inside.

—Unknown

The Declaration of Independence of the United States of America states in its preamble:

"We hold these truths to be self-evident, that all men are created equal, that they are endowed by their Creator with certain unalienable Rights, that among these are Life, Liberty and the pursuit of Happiness."

The pursuit of happiness tends to be the reason that most of us get up in the morning. We work hard to make money so that we can travel or give our kids great experiences and a good start in life. We work hard so that one day we might be able to retire and then really do what we would like to do if our health permits. Some of us love our work because we feel like we are making a difference and we find happiness in it regardless of the money. Some of us find happiness in sports and recreation. Some find it in quiet moments alone with our thoughts, while others enjoy having no thoughts at all and just love to lie brainless on a beach in the sun. Some find happiness in a good movie, a good meal, in finding an item on sale at a store, in making a meal for a sick friend.

This all encompassing pursuit to be happy is honorable and justified but also fragile. As we seek to push that happy button, it seems like there are many things that sometimes get in the way. We may lose our job. Our kids may not appreciate all the work we do in their behalf. We may get injured and not be able to play our favorite sport or might not even make the team. Those thoughts in our quiet moments may cause more stress than happiness. Our tanning on the beach may be interrupted with clouds and rain. The movies may be disappointing, the meal terrible, and the item you found on sale at a store taken by another customer right before your eyes. That hot meal for the sick friend may have to be left getting cold at the front door because nobody was home when you dropped it off.

The point is that if we seek the highs and elations of happiness at all costs, we also must be exposed to the despair and stomach wrenching that comes from unhappiness and disappointments. In the end, this teeter-totter of emotions is what most of us tend to go through as we journey through life.

I submit that the prize that is much more valuable than happiness is peace of mind.

Peace of mind comes when the actions of your life line up with the principles in which you believe. It comes when you have a long term perspective versus short term. Peace of mind is greater because it provides you stability, comfort, and the energy to persevere and keep moving forward, come what may, wherever you happen to find yourself in the spectrum of the happiness/unhappiness rainbow.

A great example for me is when my father died after a long battle with Alzheimer's disease (A.D.). I will share some stories about him later in this book but suffice it to say here that he was an incredible individual and my hero. His funeral was an emotional event for all of our family. A particular part of the funeral that I had been aware of for a long time and knew would tear me up would be the part where the lid to his casket was closed for the last time. Before the services began, we had a special gathering in a small room with just family and all said a few words. Some of us put a few things in his coffin with him and then the moment came to close the lid. I am tearing up now, six years later as I write this. It was a very sad moment. But the dread that I expected was not there. My mind was at peace that he was in a better place and that his spirit was not in that box.

This peace of mind was stronger than the sadness that I felt. It is the real prize at the end of whatever race we are running. When we live our lives according to the principles that we believe to be correct, we will have greater peace of mind. When we add a sense of deity to the mix, that there is a God that loves us, our time frames begin to stretch and our perspective broadens. Both sadness and happiness become servants to the greater master, peace of mind.

HighFive Your Life Principle

The pursuit of happiness, though important, should be accompanied also by a pursuit of peace of mind that comes when we live our lives according the principles which we believe to be correct.

CHAPTER 4

The Silver Lining in Life's Trials Is Actually Gold . . . Mine Them

May you have enough happiness to make you sweet, enough trials to make you strong, enough sorrow to keep you human, enough hope to make you happy.

—*Unknown*

Many years ago, I taught a religion course at my church for 30 to 40 single young adults (19–30 years old). We met once a week during the school year in the evening and had the summers off. I taught the class for several years and it was an extremely rewarding experience for me as I learned as much as my students did.

I almost always started my class with a short story or visible object and asked the class to teach me a lesson using the story or object I had just shared. I was always impressed at the creativity of the minds of the people in that class. We found so many interesting lessons in seemingly mundane topics that I was always behind in the designed teaching schedule. In fact, one area of study that was supposed to take me one year ended up taking two!

I have found that each of our lives has so many interesting stories and that each of those stories has hidden lessons if we just look for them. I have also found that when we find those lessons, we get a positive boost to our spirits, even if the experience recounted in the story was a tough one through which to live. When we identify the principles and look over what happened, we sometimes just have to step back and laugh at ourselves. Sometimes we have to dig deep down to discover a principle that makes us want to change or do better. The story I shared earlier regarding the tornado and my reluctance to start throwing tables around because I was not sure of my message is a good example of this. Sometimes we discover a principle that we knew already but had forgotten and just needed a little reminder. It seems that life is very generous with those reminders whether we like it or not!

Once you recognize that most events in your life can be used as teaching moments, moments where tried and true principles of life are exposed, you begin to look for them. This process of looking for and recognizing the presence of principles in your everyday living is an important way to HighFive Your Life. It allows you to accept your humanity, understand your weaknesses and yet forge ahead. It allows you to be in a position to use your experiences to help other people through their trials of life because they will find your experiences entertaining or at least interesting, and perhaps they will take your counsel a little more seriously. It allows you to be more tolerant of others and yourself as you recognize that we are all going through a very similar life experience at some fundamental level.

This book is not meant to propose a glassy-eyed happiness that glosses over the realities of a very hard world. It is more of a blue collar happiness—a happiness that is always a work in progress. It is a philosophy that espouses a sense of self worth, seeks after peace of mind that provides stability during life's ups and downs, and desires to seek out the hidden yet sustaining principles of life embedded in our everyday experiences.

I am now prepared to share with you some of my life's stories—stories that are painful, embarrassing, humorous, and touching to me. Remember that we will be looking for principles in each story that can be gleaned for our benefit. By the end of this book, I hope that you will begin to look at your own life's stories and seek out the principles that are hidden there like flakes of gold. When you discover them, you will also find it much easier and exciting to wake up every morning and HighFive Your Life.

HighFive Your Life Principle

Look for and recognize the presence of principles in your every-day living and learn to value and appreciate their importance.

Section Two

The Stories

CHAPTER 5

I've Earned Those Dimples

Golf is the only sport where, if you win 20% of the time, you're the best.
—Jack Nicklaus

Anyone who has played golf knows what it means to be frustrated. A beautiful swing yesterday that allowed you to place the ball wherever you desired on the course, today is a sneaky wretched enemy that laughs at you as you hook the ball in the water, slice the ball out of bounds, and miss a two-foot putt that should have been a "gimme."

I have played golf well during certain times of my life and have also played poorly during other times. I have caddied several times on the PGA tour for a friend that is a pro golfer. I have been hit in the neck by a golf ball, had a putter head streak by my ear after being swung by an irate golfer, taken out one sliding glass door that got in the way of my ball, hit multiple buildings, a truck, and a car. I have also hit a beautiful hole in one that took several seconds to unfold as it hit beyond the pin and gradually rolled back down the slope of the green into the hole.

Golf is a great sport! The game of golf mirrors so many of the ups and downs in our everyday lives. Each shot puts you in a new situation that requires some thought and planning to correctly hit your next shot. Sometimes you hit a perfect shot and your ball ends up with a terrible lie in the fairway. Sometimes you hit a horrible shot into the trees and the golf ball bounces back into play and lands on the green. This represents so closely what we experience in our everyday lives that I think it would be fun to use the golf ball as an object lesson to discover a very valuable life principle.

Imagine that you are in a sphere with the sphere pressing down upon you with only your hands and feet to keep it away; as if you were on the inside of a balloon with the air slowly leaking out. The outside of the sphere is smooth like a ping pong ball. Imagine that the thing that is causing this pressure—this gravity if you will—is all of the pressures of life. Let's choose four items to start with: spouse, children, home, and job.

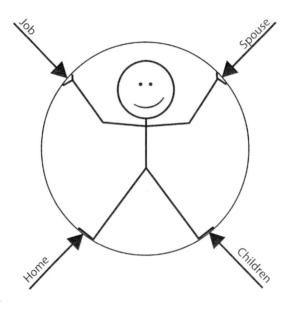

Assume that your job begins to take more and more of your time; that the "gravity" begins to come down so hard with pressure that you are required to move two hands over to cover it. That is okay for a moment, but once you do that, the spot where your other hand was (say your spouse) begins to cave in as that pressure does not let up. A dent appears.

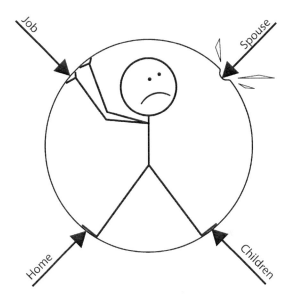

This goes on for a while until the spouse begins to make his/her feelings known, so you adjust by putting a foot that was covering the children up there and the dent at least stabilizes. However, now a dent begins to appear where your children were concerned.

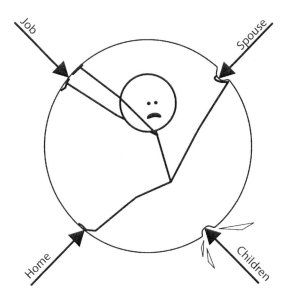

Now let's add all of the other pressures of life to the outside of the circle and begin to watch the person in the middle try to balance everything. In time, the outside of the sphere is dented all over and instead of looking like a nice new ping pong ball, it begins to look much more like a golf ball.

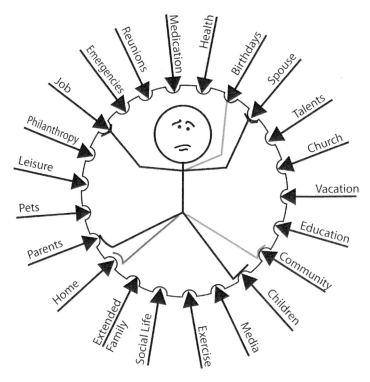

It turns out however, that a golf ball that has dents or "dimples" flies much straighter and longer than a golf ball with smooth edges.

The first golf balls were not dimpled. Over time it was noticed that a golf ball that had been scarred from use tended to fly further than the smooth ones. This is explained by the science of aerodynamics. A dimpled or scarred ball helps the ball go farther by reducing the drag on the ball. Not just a little farther—much farther!

You and I are better because of our scars of life. They are our badges of courage. They are what defines who we are and represent our struggles and successes and failures. We are meant to be dimpled! Our existence in an imperfect world with an imperfect mind and body are meant to be. I am not perfect and yet I need to find happiness and peace of mind within my own imperfections. My wife and family and friends and associates and neighbors are not perfect either and yet I still need to find happiness and peace of mind despite that reality.

I understand that there are as many as 7500 maladies that can affect your body at any given time. Think of the number of things that can go wrong with your car, home, and golf swing. There have to be at least 10,000 things that could go wrong on any given day. If we wake up late for our golf match because the alarm didn't go off, have a flat tire as we rush to the golf course, sprain our back on our first swing because we did not take time to warm up, and then dribble our first drive off the tee 70 yards, we really should be thinking that things are going pretty well! Just think of all of the other things that could have gone wrong.

Our flight through life is made better by owning our scars or imperfections. You HighFive Your Life when you can find peace of mind in the uniqueness of your "being" and are proud of the dimples that you have earned. It does not mean that we should not strive to "do" better; it does mean that we do not need to strive to "be" better.

We—you and I—are just fine the way we came.

HighFive Your Life Principle

The scars and dimples that you have earned while living your life are of great worth and part of what makes your life uniquely yours. Your flight through life will be longer and truer with your hard earned dimples.

CHAPTER 6

The Squirrel Who Would Be the Master of His Fate

Invictus
Out of the night that covers me,
Black as the pit from pole to pole,
I thank whatever gods may be
For my unconquerable soul.
In the fell clutch of circumstance
I have not winced nor cried aloud.
Under the bludgeonings of chance
My head is bloody, but unbowed.
Beyond this place of wrath and tears
Looms but the Horror of the shade,
And yet the menace of the years
Finds and shall find me unafraid.
It matters not how strait the gate,
How charged with punishments the scroll,
I am the master of my fate:
I am the captain of my soul.
—William Ernest Henley

Have you ever seen a squirrel fall from a tree? I had not until one day walking around our yard in Tangerine, Florida. I heard a rustling in the oak tree behind me and turned just in time to see a squirrel fall from about 20 feet and hit the ground with a slight thud. My mind was still processing the whole scene when the squirrel darted from his landing spot and headed for a bush near a tree. Just as he got there, a cat flashed from under a nearby car in hot pursuit but arrived too late as the squirrel escaped into the safety of the tree.

I have since pondered that scene and considered that the squirrel had three options.

Option One

> He could have gotten up slowly and shaken his fist up at the tree and exclaimed "why me . . . why does someone always push me off" . . . or "why do I always step on the rotten limb . . . why me . . . why me . . . why me"?

Option Two

> He could have lain on the ground nursing his wounds, moving each leg and arm to see where he was injured, checking his tail to make sure it was still there and able to do what a tail is supposed to do.

Option Three

> He could have run to a tree as fast as he could and scampered up to the highest limb and there, from the safety of the tree, evaluated his situation and condition, see if there were any lessons to be learned, and then returned to chasing other squirrels.

It seems to me that if the squirrel had chosen either of the first two options, he would have been eaten by the cat. I think of this falling squirrel when I see how people handle their tough situations in so many different ways. Too often, we moan and groan about the situations in which we find ourselves. We complain that due to somebody else's actions, we are here in our lousy situation. We can't wait to figure out who else is to blame because surely it could not have been our fault. Or perhaps we feel sorry for ourselves and think that we are special in our problems and that nobody else could possibly understand our situation much less care about it. We hurt and want somehow for the world to take that into account. We study our pain and resolve not to move forward but become immobilized as we concentrate on what hurts. In either case, we have placed our happiness in somebody else's control and are no longer the master of our fate. We become feline cuisine.

I like the third option best. We may not get back up in that tree and say boy that was a good fall; I really enjoyed hitting the ground at 80 MPH. We may get up in the tree and start to limp and hurt, but at least we are in the tree. At least we are in control. At least we have lived to fight another day. HighFive Your Life . . . get moving . . . get back in your tree.

HighFive Your Life Principle

Avoid looking for excuses or someone else to blame. Take the bruises that life gives you and keep moving.

CHAPTER 7

Gotta Get Over It!

*When one door of happiness closes, another opens, but often we look so long
at the closed door that we do not see the one that has been opened for us.*
                                                                    —Hellen Keller

It is important to be in control of your life even when things outside of your control occur. The desire to HighFive Your Life comes from within and is not dependent on outside circumstances which are sure to be challenging at times. It does not mean that you have to be giggling and lighthearted all of the time. It just means that you need to not get bogged down in your challenges. GOTTA GET OVER IT! Get up and move and you are on your way to finding a place to rest and gather yourself so that you can meet your challenges head on.

This is not meant to be harsh. I do not mean to minimize your pain and suffering. I do not know very many people that go through life without going through significant hardships. It is something that we all share in common at some point in our lives. Sometimes it is devastating and very difficult to understand. Sometimes our recovery is not described in hours and days but instead in weeks and years. There are things that have occurred on my life that I will never truly get over. We just need to do our best to keep moving.

One day, I was jogging on a narrow sidewalk along a road and a bird pooped on me. I could not believe it! Even when you are on the straight and narrow, poop happens. GOTTA GET OVER IT!

One day, I was enjoying a nice relaxing day on my beach chair on the beach on the west coast of Florida. My eyes were closed and so I did not see the kids sneak up and throw handfuls of sand all over me. When it hit with such a splattering thud, I instantly opened my eyes but to my surprise, there were no kids around me at all and the sand was not sand at all. The huge pelican flying overhead just decided to give me a little gift. Even when you are minding your own business and not in anybody else's way, poop happens. GOTTA GET OVER IT!

One day, the week before our preseason high school football game my senior year, I hit someone's helmet with my hand as I was throwing the ball and broke my thumb. We were slated to go very far that year and I was devastated. I missed the first four games of the season and in the first game in which I was finally allowed to play, I got knocked out. We won our next three games but in the last game of the season lost to our cross-county rival for the first time in over ten years. I threw four interceptions in that game. Sometimes our personal agendas just don't work out the way we thought they would. GOTTA GET OVER IT!

One day, a girl that I had dated told me she was marrying her old boyfriend. I thought I was okay with the news until the day of the wedding approached when I started feeling like I really blew it. I called from my house on the wedding day to speak with her and expressed my love. Her bridesmaid tried to stop me. As the hour of the wedding drew near, I curled up in agony on the carpet at my home. It was a horrible gut wrenching pain. I even considered showing up to stop the wedding. Thank goodness I was not that much of a jerk. Later, I found the true love of my life and we have been married for over 23 years and have four beautiful children. I am sure the other girl is happy, too. GOTTA GET OVER IT!

One day, while playing little league, a bossy older girl chased me down and beat me up. I thought she was kidding as she chased me around the bleacher area, but she wasn't. As I headed home crying, she planted her foot in my back and ripped my shirt off. GOTTA GET OVER IT! I think I could take her out now; well, maybe not. I hope she doesn't read this.

One Friday, the 100-year storm hit Kissimmee and tore down trees and created flooding. To make it worse, we had the biggest weekend event planned in the history of Water Mania, our water park. A huge Central Florida hospital had booked a catered weekend event and we were expecting several thousand people. In the wee hours of the morning on Saturday as my GM and I watched the fierce wind blow over trees in the park, we knew the event would be a bust. We were correct. Instead of making money that weekend we cleaned and repaired. Sometimes our plans just don't pan out. GOTTA GET OVER IT!

One day, my Uncle Mel came from California to visit my mom and dad. An older man, he settled in the bathtub for a nice warm bath. To his surprise and near heart failure, a snake poked his head through the overflow hole by his feet. He jumped out of that tub like an Olympic star. He survived that event and now it is just a fun story. GOTTA GET OVER IT!

One day my mother-in-law was sick and I was the only one around to help. As she walked through her living room she became nauseous. Trying to be the son-in-law from heaven, I rushed to the kitchen and got her a bowl, showing up just in time. Only then did I realize I had brought her a colander instead of a bowl. GOTTA GET OVER IT! She still loves me. . . . doesn't she?

One day in college, I went to my friend's class to meet him. It was in an art class and I waited at the door for him to finish. There was a window in the door and as I peered through looking for him I noticed that the class had a naked mannequin on a slowly rotating table in the middle of the desks. I continued to look for my friend through the window in the door and all of a sudden the mannequin moved! She was alive! I was stunned and quickly got away from the door. Did anybody see me? Did my looking for my friend look like I was gawking? To this day I claim my innocence. Sometimes we just look like we are doing something wrong. GOTTA GET OVER IT! . . . and no, I did not drop my class and switch to art.

One day after work, I went to work out at a local gym. Through college I spent a lot of time working out, but at this time in my life I had not been in a long while. I settled in the men's room and took my time to change into my workout clothes. There was nobody there. As I came out of the restroom, I noticed that I had actually been casually getting ready in the women's restroom. The painted sign "Women" was partially blocked by a wall so that all I saw was ". . . men." I was so sure of where I was that if a woman would have come in, I would have told her she was in the wrong place. I also could have easily been unpresentable when she did come in and then who knows in which jail I would have ended up. Sometimes when you are just plain stupid it is hard to do, but you still GOTTA GET OVER IT!

My list could go on and on and on, as I am sure your list could . . . at least I am thinking that your list is as long as mine . . . isn't it?

HighFive Your Life Principle

Grit your teeth and GET OVER IT! Just gotta do it.

CHAPTER 8

Ouch . . . My Feet Are Burning!

One of the most difficult things everyone has to learn is that for your entire life you must keep fighting and adjusting if you hope to survive. No matter who you are or what your position is you must keep fighting for whatever it is you desire to achieve.

—*NFL Coach George Allen*

One year a very dear friend invited me to go to Hawaii to attend a ten-day motivational seminar. His wife did not want to go and he had paid for two people so he invited me. I had been working on my health and running a little so I agreed. We met in San Francisco and flew to Hawaii together.

The lessons and talks and training of those days in beautiful Hawaii all led up to the grand finale when we would walk on hot coals. I honestly was not too worried because I had seen a TV special regarding walking on hot coals and remembered that there was some science that explained why it did not burn your feet. Also, there were 1500 or so other convention goers seeking this life improving motivation; surely the organizers would not put us all through something that really was dangerous.

At any rate, I did not think about it much until the day came when it was time to challenge the red hot coals. The morning began with speeches and meditation focused on the upcoming event. We all marched out to the outdoor venue where the fire was ceremoniously lit. We were all encouraged to write down on a piece of paper a characteristic or flaw or habit that we wanted to get rid of and then cast it into the fire, which

I did. We marched back to the convention facility and continued with our mental preparation.

I have to admit again, that I was not very worried about the whole thing but went along with the buildup. We were told to create our "mantras," which I did. These were to be repeated as you got prepared to walk across the coals. Again, I participated but did not get too enthusiastic with my preparation. My mantra was "heart, might, mind, and soul" and as I recited these words out loud, I would use my fists and arms to hit or indicate my heart, might, mind, and soul in a ritualistic motion.

The time came for us to return to the fires that had been lit in the morning. This time the scene was a little different. It was dark outside. There were drums beating in the background. Lines were forming in front of 20 or so long thin coal beds which glowed a bright reddish-orange in the darkened sky. As I recall, we were setting some kind of record (probably just for this seminar) and they had made them a little longer, about 43 feet or so.

For the first time, my heart began to race a little. I started getting a little nervous and as my position in line gradually got closer and closer to the front, I found that I started putting a little more emphasis on my mantra: heart, might, mind, and soul . . . heart, might, mind, and soul . . . heart, might, mind, and soul. Now I was near the front . . . then I was next in line . . . heart, might, mind, and soul . . . heart, might, mind, and soul . . . poured out of my mouth with greater intensity and frequency.

And then it was my turn . . . heart, might, mind, and soul . . . heart, might, mind, and soul . . . I was scared and nervous and tense and . . . all of a sudden the attendant stopped me. I was surprised and a little taken back but then saw the reason why they had stopped me. I had to stand there while they brought out the wheel barrow and shovel and piled more fresh hot coals on my track. How they had determined that it was not hot enough already my heart, might, mind, and soul will never know, but somehow, someone who was not walking on the coals decided that my track needed to be a little more challenging!

It was my turn and there was no way to go but forward. I had a line behind me. The drums were beating. There was a surreal intensity in the air, so off I went. I remember taking two steps and as I began to take the third step, the toes on my right foot began to burn. I remember being surprised at the pain. I was burning! What was I thinking? Why would I suppose in my right mind that I should expect to get a different result than the one I get when I grill out in my back yard? TV show or not, what was I thinking? Why would I really expect any result other than burning flesh?

I then learned the value of all of the build up and preparation. This was the principle embedded in this experience. My immediate impulse was to jump off the coals. It was a natural reaction and would have surely been the one I pursued had I not been preparing with the mantra: heart, might, mind, and soul . . . heart, might, mind and soul. I continued forward with a quick but non-panicked pace and crossed the coals.

The elation I felt at the end of that walk was unexpected. I felt a natural high. I had accomplished something that I had not anticipated was going to be so hard and later was so grateful for the preparation that I had been given by those that had done it before.

Often in our lives we just jump out of the coals too soon. When the kitchen gets hot we just check out and move on to something that isn't so hard. Part of life's joy is to challenge it. If you do not prepare yourself you will often find that the challenges of life just seem too hard. On the other hand, if you prepare yourself mentally, physically, emotionally, and spiritually for what lies ahead, you will find that you are more likely able to meet those same challenges and succeed.

My father sent me a letter in college that makes more sense to me now than when I was younger. He encouraged me to keep moving ahead despite the pressure. The latter part of the letter is the part that is dearest to me and causes the most reflection.

"However, Mother and I often discuss whether we have made it look to[o] easy or not. Love of family, country and God and the willingness to challenge life are what make it all so much fun and worthwhile."

Notice that he was not real big on stationary.

April 6, 1976

Hi Gary,

I saw this article in Sunday's paper and that it was appropriate to your questions on this subject last week. We did enjoy your phone call ... on it. It looks like maybe you might be getting it all put together there at Princeton. I realize that the pressure must be tremendous, but remember that you're competing academically with some of the best in the world. If you can keep that in perspective and the importance of young people like yourself to our overall way of life and this great country of ours, somehow it makes it all worthwhile. We appreciate the fact that you enjoy your home so much & do such a good job of letting us share in that feeling. However, mother and I often discuss whether we have made it look too easy or not. Love of family, country and God, and the willingness to challenge life are what make it all so much fun & worthwhile.

Good luck on all that you're doing there this week and will be looking forward to hearing from you. —

... but .50? this wk. your hom. D.V.

SOUTHERN CULVERT
STEEL – ALUMINUM – CONCRETE
A DIVISION OF
ST REGIS PAPER COMPANY
P. O. Box 457
Pinellas Park
Florida 33565
St. Pete 813/544-8811
Ft. Pierce 305/464-4400
Plant City 813/752-5138
NATIONAL PIPE COMPANY
FORMERLY
CULVERT MANUFACTURING COMPANY

Now as a parent, I also worry about making things look too easy for my children. I sometimes fear that I have not prepared them enough to grab life and challenge it. It doesn't take long though to realize that my children, like everyone else, are going to get thrust into the challenges of life whether they want to or not and whether they are prepared or not. We tend to do better, however, if we prepare ourselves for the fight that is coming our way.

You can HighFive Your Life by preparing for the challenges of life and meeting them head on. Below is a picture of my father with those wise words from his letter to a young and clueless college kid . . . me. Get prepared. Go for it. Challenge Life!

HighFive Your Life Principle

Prepare for and embrace the challenges of life. You will find greater joy as you meet them head on.

Challenge Life

"Love of family, country and God, and the willingness to challenge life are what makes it all so fun and worthwhile"

Robert Larson (dad) 1929 - 2005

CHAPTER 9

Believe in Yourself Regardless

Keep away from those who try to belittle your ambitions. Small people always do that, but the really great make you believe that you too can become great.
—Mark Twain

I loved my high school sports days. We won just enough football games to make those crisp Autumn Friday nights something that my friends and I can still enjoy talking about many years later. Thirty-five years later, we can't always remember our kids' birthdays but we know who caught or dropped a pass and what the scores were in many of those games!

I was recruited as a quarterback (QB) to Princeton University. I had no Ivy League ambitions. I excelled in school, but mentally I was stuck somewhere between assuming that I would go to a local college and having no idea of what I was going to do.

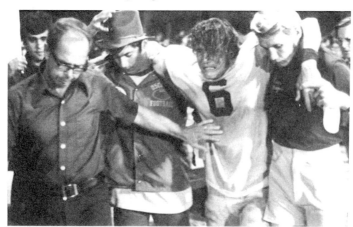

My father (on left) helping me off the field after getting knocked out in a high school game.

Thank goodness for alumni recruiters. An older gentleman from South Florida made Princeton aware of my football potential and it was arranged for me to visit the campus in Princeton, New Jersey. What an impressive and life changing visit! The campus and history were both overwhelming. I knew that this was the place for me. I was so sure that I did not apply to a single other school. In retrospect, that was perhaps more than just a little naïve but reflects just how confident I was. I was accepted to enter with the freshmen class in the fall of 1975.

As an alumnus, I have the opportunity to conduct interviews of high school seniors applying to Princeton in my local area. I remember one interview where the candidate was explaining with amazing zeal how much he enjoyed studying elliptical orbits. I remember sitting there as I was taking notes, trying to remember how to spell "elliptical." Thank goodness I don't have to apply again in this century.

It was a great day when I got my acceptance letter. The coaches sent a summer training schedule to help me be ready for football season. I lifted weights and ran and trained with great anticipation of playing college football. As the date to report to fall practice approached, I worked out with my high school football team, the Osceola Kowboys. Unbelievably, just a few days before heading to Princeton, I suffered a shoulder injury that left my throwing arm completely useless. I could hardly lift it much less throw a football. I assumed that it would heal quickly but it was not to be.

The first day of college football practice was extremely competitive: new faces, everybody sizing everybody up. During warm ups we ran high stepping sprints and to my utter dismay, my right foot suffered a stress fracture and I was out. Just like that, one of their two blue chip quarterback recruits shows up to camp unable to throw a football and breaks his foot on the first day.

It was extremely depressing. I completed the season as more of a tag along on the sidelines than a serious football player. Most of the season, I could not even practice. I knew that my sophomore year would be better.

The next year I showed up to camp healthy and ready to go. I had less experience than the others but I felt confident. It did not take long though to find out that I was not as prepared as I needed to be. There were at least ten other QBs vying for the varsity spot. One of the other QBs was another sophomore whom I will call John. He was the other blue chip QB that came to Princeton as a freshman. In retrospect, maybe they told all of us we were blue chip prospects. I don't know, but man oh man, could he throw a beautiful spiral. It was perfect. Mine on the other hand, was more of a brute force spiral that traveled through the air to the spot I desired more because of my strength than my technique in throwing. John's spiral was poetry; it was like it wanted to get to its destination all on its own, without needing to be forced by some brute arm strength.

On the second or third day of camp we were doing two-a-day practices and sleeping and eating at Jadwin Gym. I will never forget the practice that affected my life forever. I was in the huddle calling the play. I was hesitant and not really getting it right for some reason. John stepped into the huddle and with a slight brush of his arm, pushed me aside and said something to the effect of "I'll take this huddle." I let him do it. I was numb and in shock. Years later, I do not blame John for doing what he did. We were all competing for one spot. I am just mad at myself for allowing him to do it.

After practice I tried to call my dad but could not reach him. During my entire high school career I played football with coaches and players and friends building me up as a great football player and here in just a few seconds, a competitor brushed me aside like I was nothing. Insecurities, which I did not know I had, surfaced like an exploding sore. It was ugly.

I went in to see the coach after lunch and through my tears said that I needed to quit or change to running back. I felt like I needed something that didn't require as much thinking and so that afternoon I came out to practice as a fullback. I will never forget that practice. I was a running QB anyway so it was not that hard to pick it up. Coach called a play where I got the ball and I headed through the line. I guess a young linebacker was thinking that we were not running full speed or he didn't know that my adrenaline was pretty high and I ran right over him. It was a big deal and got a lot of yells of approval. I now feel a little sorry for him, but I will always be thankful that he helped me get the coach's attention. I got a lot of play time that year as a running back and thought I was satisfied with my football experience at that position. My junior year I was the starting fullback and started every game from then on except when I had an injury.

Author carrying the football at Princeton (please don't fumble!)

Something was nagging me, though. All of the other QBs that had intimidated me so much were either no longer on the team or not doing that well. I began to feel that I had made a mistake by not sticking it out. When I returned for my senior year, I wanted to try out for QB but it was too late. We had a new head coach and the QBs were now all a year younger than I was. I started as fullback and did some good things but the truth is, I was never really a very good fullback. I was just fast enough and strong enough to show up and make a difference, but I never had the skills to dominate in that position. It took me years after I graduated to get over the internal hurt and feeling that I had left something on the table. I was a good fullback but always felt that I could have been a great QB.

Perhaps it is best to never know the truth of whether I would have been good or not because the one halfback pass that I threw as a senior fullback against Yale was intercepted!

The HighFive Your Life principle that I learned from this experience is to never stop believing in yourself. When we put time constraints on our success or progress, we sometimes get down on ourselves for not being what we thought we ought to be by a certain time. I should have had a much better grasp of reality and known that with ten other QBs competing for the job, it was just going to take time—time for me to learn the job, time for the coaches to see what I could do, time for me to get more confidence. My expectation was not realistic and so I doubted myself instead of embracing the challenge.

I may never have been a great QB but I shortchanged myself by not going through the process of discovering that for myself. The process of discovering your personal gifts is a very valuable tool that you lose if you stop short of giving it your all over an extended period of time, including the time when you are the only one left believing in you. That is the most valuable time and the time when you learn and progress the most. Do not deny yourself the opportunity to believe in yourself when nobody else does. My commitment to myself is to never let that happen to me again.

HighFive Your Life Principle

Never stop believing in yourself, especially when you are the only one left that does.

CHAPTER 10

Impatience Is Not the Enemy to Patience

Patience is the mother of will.

—*Gurdjieff*

I got married when I was 31 years old. Marriage and a family had always been part of the plan for me but intensified when I returned from my church mission at the age of 24. I was starting a two-year graduate program and was ready to settle down and get serious about raising a family. I dated many wonderful ladies and once was actually engaged for a few days, but it just never worked out.

As the years went by, I would go through phases of massive travel around the state and country to do my best to find that special someone, followed by periods of just leaving it alone and immersing myself in work, thinking my marriage would never happen. Those were trying years for me because I wanted it so badly. I was impatient but never gave up.

In 1987, at the age of 30, I attended a Christmas party hosted by the local tourism bureau. It was like many of the other parties I had attended but this time my sister-in-law introduced me to somebody that turned out to be pretty special. Joey Forrest was an outstanding sales manager for a local major tourist attraction in Central Florida. Our first encounter left us each with our own impression of the other. She thought I was drunk (I don't drink) and I thought she was chubby (what a dummy I was). Despite our misgivings about the other, we each visited the other's tourist attraction and shared lunch. I then asked her out on our first date, which was on Saturday, March 12, 1988. The entry in my journal in part reads:

I took Randy home and rushed by the car wash and vacuumed out the car [I had a dog]. I bought some deodorizers (3 kinds) and some sun glasses and hustled home. I showered and raced off but was still 15 minutes late to Joey's home. I'm about ready to describe the near perfect date. We met Donna and Randy and went to the tennis tournament at the Grand Cypress. It was fantastic. The weather was perfect and the intensity was inspiring. We then went out to the lake house and went for a great long boat ride. We BBQued and then Donna and Randy left. What transpired next had the setting for a great movie. We went out on the houseboat and danced to soft music. Joey is a great girl. We stayed out there for four hours. I even took the guitar.

Within a few months we knew we were in love and were married on Sept 17, 1988. On the day of our wedding my journal entry begins with:

What can I say? It's finally here. Today is the day I have dreamed about forever.

The years of my waiting—albeit impatiently—for this perfect moment to finally arrive paid off in great dividends. Those dividends of course are our 23 years of marriage and our children who are the joy of our lives. I am the luckiest man alive.

Robbie, Taylor, Gary, Allie, Calahan, Joey

I always find it interesting that the times we need patience the most are the times we want it the least. We want our results now and will do almost anything to make it happen. As mentioned in the previous chapter, if I'd had patience as a football quarterback, I would have found out just how good I could have been. In our society today, the virtue of patience is found lacking in a significant way.

I have not done much research, but my guess is that patience is a concept that has been discussed in religious and philosophical writings for eons. It is interesting that the Bible is full of verses that discuss patience. In James 1:3–4 in the King James Version of the New Testament it says the following:

> *Vs 3 Knowing this that the trying of your faith worketh patience.*
> *Vs 4 But let patience have her perfect work, that ye may be perfect and entire, wanting nothing.*

In these two verses we are reminded that the trying of our faith "worketh" patience and that we should "let" patience have her perfect work in us. I have to admit that I have pondered this teaching many times because patience is not a virtue which comes naturally for me. I have to work hard to "let" patience find some place in my daily life. A person that is being patient is usually being denied something that they want or need.

As hard as I have to work at it, I am still intrigued by what is taking place inside an individual that allows a "perfect work" to take place. I think another way to say perfect work might be to say completed work. The verse says that you can become perfect and entire, wanting nothing. What exactly happens to a person that is being patient? Do they develop new skills such as self discipline? Do they mature in a way that comes only through having patience? As I said in the beginning of this chapter, I always find it interesting that we need patience when we want it the least.

Several things come to mind when I think of a patient person. In the movies we always see the wise old man pictured as a quiet, pensive person, someone who is not in a hurry—someone who is not shouting. My grandfather used to quote the following:

The wise old owl sat in an oak.
The more he saw, the less he spoke.
The less he spoke, the more he heard.
Why can't we all be like that bird?

P-Pa Dossey

I am not sure where the quote comes from but we had his three daughters sign this picture when they were in their eighties to give out at a family reunion. I love its message. I took the picture of the owl on an oak tree in my backyard.

It would seem that the very essence of patience has a time element that seems to slow things down a little. Perhaps as we slow things down, we gain perspective. Perhaps we listen better. Perhaps we see a bigger picture.

Another interesting byproduct of being patient is that it tends to affect those around us in a calming way. In the Bible we are counseled to be wise as serpents and harmless as doves (Mathew 10:16). In my opinion, a person is "wise and harmless" when they take into consideration someone else's well-being above their own.

It is human nature, especially in type-A personalities, to become competitive or dominate when confronted by another competitive or domineering personality. Often this creates a venue for non-productive, forceful, turf-defending conversations. On the other hand, a person who is "wise and harmless" may create an environment for very productive conversations that are uplifting and result in problem solving, clearer vision, and positive traction on a given problem.

On the first take this may seem like a style of life management that works only in church. My football coaches, whom I still worship, were not "harmless" types at all. They scared me to death. They yelled at me and pushed me to be my best. Aren't we thankful that an army sergeant doesn't slow down and discuss every little ache and pain of his solders at boot camp? It just wouldn't work. So, as in most things, there is a time and a place and a balance for everything. If my football coach treated his wife like he treated us at practice, he would have not been a very happy man for long. There are places and environments where the team understands that discipline, direction, and instruction are not going to be delivered with a bouquet of flowers and some chocolates. This is an exception to the rule and one that everyone should know and understand and have that expectation going in.

I like this quote by Marvin Ashton:

> *Perhaps the greatest charity comes when we are kind to each other, when we don't judge or categorize someone else, when we simply give each other the benefit of the doubt or remain quiet. Charity is accepting someone's differences, weaknesses, and shortcomings; having patience with someone who has let us down; or resisting the impulse to become offended when someone doesn't handle something the way we might have hoped. Charity is refusing to take advantage of another's weakness and being willing to forgive someone who has hurt us. Charity is expecting the best of each other.*
>
> *None of us need one more person bashing or pointing out where we have failed or fallen short. Most of us are already well aware of the areas in which we are weak. What each of us does need is family, friends, employers, and brothers and sisters who support us, who have the patience to teach us, who believe in us, and who believe we're trying to do the best we can, in spite of our weaknesses. Whatever happened to giving each other the benefit of the doubt? Whatever happened to hoping that*

another person would succeed or achieve? Whatever happened to rooting for each other?

—*May 1992,* Ensign, *"The Tongue Can Be A Sharp Sword."*

Would this work in a business environment where productivity is critical? Like all great principles, there is often a balance that needs to be struck between it and other principles such as the "law of the harvest" and "chop wood carry water." It is a basis from which you need to build ways to be productive, and building people around you generally is a good first step. It is not lowering a standard or expectation. In fact, if done properly, it is the propellant that will increase your productivity tremendously. I have found that it is not an easy skill to master as our desire to get things done now is generally the most significant driving force. Over the course of years with my staff, friends, children, and spouse I have had episodes of great progress with this, and other times when I have shown a lack of maturity. However, it is a goal that is worthy of our best efforts.

It is interesting that the scripture verse that follows the two that I began with states:

> *Vs 5 If any of you lack wisdom, let him ask of God, that giveth to all men liberally, and upbraideth not; and it shall be given him.*

In other words, if we are to let patience have her perfect work in us, it does not mean that we should sit like bumps on a log waiting for something good to happen. In this quiet time, we are to ask God for wisdom. If you do not believe in God, perhaps it is a time to ask friends and family for wisdom. We should be like the owl and speak less and listen more and then we will begin to gain a perspective that we would never get going 100 MPH to get to the results we desire. Being patient is a skill that is developed through self-discipline. It sometimes involves pain and tears and moments of loneliness, but it is the way to inner peace and control, and most often the result is that you are wiser in how you handle the problems before you.

There is really only one thing that can rob you of the benefit of patience, and that is to quit. That is the true enemy to patience. When we reach a point and we say "whatever" or "to heck with it" and we stop the process of trying to understand and of seeking wisdom, that is the only time the virtues of patience are lost. It is the very act of trying to be patient where the true value is found.

You can HighFive Your Life by pushing through the trials, asking for wisdom as you go. Indeed, letting patience have her perfect work in you might make you a star of the next wise-old-man movie, or it might just help you save yourself and your loved ones from unnecessary pains that could be avoided with just the right amount of being "wise and harmless."

HighFive Your Life Principle

Realize your true potential by not quitting on patience. The true enemy to patience is not impatience, but instead quitting or giving up.

Chapter 11

Not Knowing When to Quit
Is a Great Virtue

Pain is temporary. Quitting lasts forever.

—*Lance Armstrong*

In the spring of 1975, while still in high school, I had a varsity baseball game. It was just your normal everyday scene that is replicated thousands of times across the country each spring. This was a little different for me because I was a senior with only a few short months before I would graduate. I had a fairly successful baseball career and maybe was feeling a little too good about myself. In the course of the game, it was obvious to me that I was having an off day and since I was a senior and such a "good" player, I actually went to the coach and asked him to take me out of the game. I had never done that before and I do not remember much after that except when I got home.

As I walked through the front door, my dad was crossing the foyer in front of me and I casually related what had happened as a friend would do to a friend. Of course, my mom and dad were my best supporters so I expected an understanding nod from him. I was stunned when he started yelling at me and let me have it with me just barely inside the house. He told me not to start anything that I was not going to finish. He shouted many other things that I don't remember now, but I will never forget those few seconds with my dad. It was clear that I had hit a nerve.

Dad would leave for work early in the morning and on occasion, would leave a note for me to find before I went to school. One such note regarded giving my very best effort on the JV basketball team. It follows:

Dear Gary !!   Fri

Remember how coach, Granata handled you during last year's basketball season. In my analysis, he made you know that you had to put out a 100% effort to make the team. When you did this he let you play. When you put out 90% effort he could recognize it and it angered him and you would be benched. His respect for you was so great that he would not allow you to put out less than total effort. As you develop as an athlete and a man you must learn to recognize this in yourself. On every play tonight see if you have given 100%.

As I have grown older, I have appreciated the wisdom and energy in his counsel. So many good things have happened in my life simply because I did not quit. What we learn in sports can often be wise counsel also for our daily lives. As with most principles, there is a time and place and balance that must be struck to use the principle of quitting or nor quitting properly. A couple of examples of not quitting are offered below.

Around 1992, with the help of our mother, my brother and sister and I developed a neckwear business on the side, with ties that were meant to be conversational in nature. The brand was called "Lousy." We came up with 40 designs and my brother took the lead to try and get the company up and running. The trouble was that we developed a product that in reality was lousy. When my brother went to a menswear shop to try and sell some, the owner told him that there were three things wrong with his ties: the design, the material, and the price! There's not much else that could be wrong with a tie.

We found however that several of the designs with religious themes placed in Christian bookstores by our sister started moving; slowly, but moving nonetheless. We rethought our strategy, changed the name of the company first to Ties Made Right, and then to Eagles Wings, and began to push the Inspirational ties more. The company still struggled and my brother and I bought my sister's shares and limped along. The breakthrough came when he attended a Christian Retail Show and found that there was a lot of demand for the product. It stayed a one or two man show for several years and then began to expand into licensed products. At one point in 2008, the Larson and Eagles Wings brands of neckwear were in many major retailers including over 3000 Walmart stores. The licenses included many colleges, the NFL, and MLB.

This success comes from my brother's leadership and his great staff. There have been many times over the almost 20 years of history when we could have quit. Instead, he found another way, he pondered, he was patient and learned from his mistakes. Today Eagles Wings sells a variety of products to retailers and customers all over the world. It was the right thing to keep fighting and changing to find our way. You can HighFive Your Life by pressing forward and not quitting while seeking solutions to your challenges.

Another personal example of not quitting has been with my wife. I did not get married until I was 31 years old. She was 27 and a very successful sales manager at a Central Florida attraction. She was confident, beautiful, and very smart, despite what some may conclude was an error in her judgment to marry me. We had four children in five years and moved our young family to a farm in Apopka, Florida. She was a cul-de-sac woman but allowed me the opportunity to live a dream on this farm with cows, chickens, and even a pig that lived under the house.

One evening after the children were asleep, we were lying in bed talking about the day. I began to explain to her what a great husband I was. I listed all of the things that I had done for her and went on and on. She finally interrupted me and said something to the effect of "Gary, I know that among men you are at the top of the list but the whole species of men is so low that you could be at the top and you would still be way down here." That is a classic example of the kind of woman I married: loving but blunt and direct.

Much later in life, my wife and I got into an argument that lasted several days. It was one of those disputes that had no apparent good ending possible. We discussed parting in a way that was very real. The intensity of the situation can only be known by those that have lived it. After several days of this, as I contemplated what I considered my righteous position, I realized that what I wanted most was to grow old with her. It hit me in such a profound way and I realized that the issue that was causing our situation was really not an issue at all in comparison to the possibility of living without her for the rest of my life. The situation immediately calmed and dissipated.

It is an example of where quitting would have been the wrong thing to do. The process of patience, though intense and not feeling like patience at all, allowed my head to find wisdom and perspective. Instead of confirming that I was just another man species, I became something more; we became something more. Had I quit, I would have lost the treasure of my life.

You can HighFive Your Life by sticking to the tasks at hand. Often times, we stop just because we are tired and can't see the finish line. If we knew it was right around the corner we could probably muster enough strength to get going. By exercising patience, we can perhaps gain more perspective on just where the finish line is and whether our efforts are placed in the right direction. When you work your way through this process you are giving your life the attention that it deserves. You are HighFiving Your Life. You are working towards a finish line of your choosing and you are feeling the value of your effort even if it is a long race. Your finish line is clear in your mind. Achieving your goal is worth the pain. You keep going.

HighFive Your Life Principle

Don't quit or give up. Force yourself to keep going while always looking for ways to solve your challenges. Answers will appear as you press forward.

CHAPTER 12

Knowing When to Quit
Is Also a Great Virtue

Courage is going from failure to failure without losing enthusiasm.
—Winston Churchill

So is it ever right to quit? There are times when you make a bad decision that will require you to change course. It may be the wrong job or relationship or it may just be time to move on. "Not Quitting" is a principle that should make you evaluate and struggle to find the correct path, which generally takes you somewhere past the point when someone less committed would say "whatever." Knowing when to quit is when you have pushed and pushed and every ounce of your soul finally says that it is time to move on. I think that this is a solid principle of life also.

Kissimmee Kahootchie is a great example of this. In preparing for our annual company party at which management generally grilled the meat, we put together a simple but incredibly good tasting marinade. It was so good that later we decided that we should make and sell it. I hired a good friend and we started experimenting but could never quite rediscover the great tasting marinade that we had at the company party. Not to be deterred, we created a new marinade that we also liked, along with a whole family of sauces and rubs. We created Kissimmee Kahootchie and Stone Aged Products. Our theme was simple: early man created the sauce to impress early woman and it was so good that it was the main reason why dinosaurs went extinct. I still love that theme and may try and resurrect it one day. Of course if I do, it would probably be the reason my wife would choose to make me extinct!

We worked hard to get our product on the shelves and in front of people to try. Over the course of the next three years, we attended trade shows and made sales pitches, created recipes, and gave product away. We worked our tails off to make this product successful. The end result was that we lost a lot of money and finally decided that it just was not worth the effort that it would have taken to get it off the ground. I have never given up on the concept, but conceded that it was probably better to use our very limited capital in other directions.

Still I found it hard to quit. We tried to repackage the rubs and use them in the industry where our Inspirational ties were selling successfully. Our Southern Rub became "Salt of the Earth." We changed a couple of others things and redesigned the packaging complete with a scripture quote on each bottle. We sold very few.

In an act of complete desperation and not wanting to waste all of the empty bottles that we had left over, I created a label that did not need any real product inside. It was called Gator Gas.

We put a few in our gift shops that had a lot of foreign tourists who I thought would love the perfect gift to take home from Florida. My peers were not surprised to find out that we did not sell one of them! Of course, I think we just did a poor job in merchandising, and maybe one day I will bring that product back also!

A HighFive Your Life principle is that sometimes it is okay to quit and change directions when it is obvious that you have better options somewhere else and you just need to make a change. This is a different type of change than just giving up after only minimal effort. As you seek wisdom and guidance you will eventually know if and when it is time to chart another course.

HighFive Your Life Principle

When you have pushed and pushed and tried hard to make it work but every ounce of your soul finally says that it is time to move on . . . that is ok.

CHAPTER 13

A Short Story Regarding Number One

By prevailing over all obstacles and distractions, one may unfailingly arrive at his chosen goal or destination.

—*Christopher Columbus*

When we moved our family to Apopka, Florida, we moved into an old frame house that had not been lived in for several years. We spent a lot of money and time getting it back up to some acceptable living standard. One of the things we did was correct an interesting bathroom layout. As soon as you walked in the door of the house, there was a bathroom on your immediate left with two toilets side by side. We still do not know why it was built like that unless the previous owners liked to play checkers instead of read. We liked the country living, but that was a little too much for even us!

One day after we had moved in and this bathroom was changed to a one toilet establishment, my wife and I noticed a pool of liquid on the floor around the base of the toilet. As we had three small boys, the investigative work was not all that complicated. However, when we finally did get one to confess, the reason behind the puddle was a surprise.

It seems that our youngest son Taylor was standing there taking care of number one when he spied a spider crawling on the wall next to the toilet. He simply did what any other country boy would do—he tried to shoot it down! Needless to say, we knew we had some work to do as parents.

The HighFive Your Life principle to be gleaned from this story is to take care of the business at hand and do not be persuaded to participate in the many meaningless distractions that are around us. If you aim at the wrong target, whether you hit or miss, you may have a momentary high but still have a mess to clean up.

HighFive Your Life Principle

Focus on the task at hand . . . or don't tinkle on the wall . . . you choose.

CHAPTER 14

Don't Chase the Little Walking Rear Ends

My thoughts before a big race are usually pretty simple. I tell myself: Get out of the blocks, run your race, stay relaxed. If you run your race, you'll win . . . channel your energy. Focus.

—Carl Lewis

I n the previous chapters, I discussed when to stay the course and when to change it. If you are able to keep the finish line in your vision you have a better chance to make the determination whether the value of your course is worth the pain. Sometimes we look around us and decide that someone else is on a different course that we like a little better. They are richer or more successful at something that is of interest to us. While it is okay to be motivated by watching and sometimes studying successful people, you should not get pushed to enter a race that you either do not want to run or that you want to run at a different speed. When that happens, you are inevitably running someone else's race, complete with their definitions of victory. This may eventually create situations in your life that cause unnecessary pain and grief.

In my early 40s, a friend of mine told me that I needed to lose weight or I was going to die. He had his own issues to work out, so we made a pact that each day I would run as long as he took care of his issue each day. That turned into a life style change for me and before I stopped, I had run at least 900 days without missing a single day. It did not matter whether I was on a vacation, at a truck stop, or in a hotel, I laced up my shoes and jogged at least a little to keep my commitment. It no longer mattered whether my friend kept his commitment or not. He had changed my life. I only stopped the night that my father almost passed away in the hospital. I could have done my run, but as I sat talking with my mom in the hospital parking lot that night I just forgot, and that stopped my streak.

Before it was over though, my friend suggested we run a half marathon in Orlando. In the past, I had hated running long distances. By this time however, I had discovered a pace that made running actually seem enjoyable. I really looked forward to it. Many people that saw me on the side of the road would comment later on in the week that they had seen me walking. I told them thanks but that was me running, not walking!

I decided that I wanted to give this half marathon a try. I was nervous as I gathered with my friend and another 1000 people in downtown Orlando the morning of the event. I told my friend that he did not have to stay with me. My only goal was to finish the 13-plus miles without walking and that I needed to run at my own pace. He was okay with that and as soon as we took off he began to pull away.

I settled into a rhythm that moved me along the course, not fast but steady. People were everywhere and were passing me on the left and the right, but that was fine because I wanted to run my race at my speed. Around the second or third mile, however, the fast walkers began to catch me. This was an insult. Not only did I have to watch their small little rear ends go by me, but they went by me ever so slowly. It seemed like forever before they finally moved on and gave my eyes a rest. The big insult, however, occurred later in the race when a guy with a metal leg came by. I thought that it really wasn't fair to not have muscles in that prosthesis that were getting really tired like mine! But I held my pace and ran my race. (This is only meant to show the contrast of how slow I really was and not to disparage the guy running the race with a prosthesis. I hold that guy in very high regard).

Around the 10th mile or so, a tanned little 70 or 80 or 120-year-old woman came by me. I couldn't believe it. I was getting pretty tired by this stage and I just watched her go by, probably with unkind thoughts in my head. To my surprise, I soon found that she had slowed down or walked and I passed her. It was not long before she started running and passed me again. Soon I saw her on the side of the road talking with somebody in their yard and that's when I made a commitment that I was not going to lose to grandma! I picked it up a notch. I knew that I was getting close to the end of the race. I had never run this far in my life. I am here to tell you that I whooped her and she never passed me again! Whooo Hoooo! I whooped that 80 year old lady! I am the man! Isn't everyone proud of me?

I was so happy that she did not pass me again. The only problem I had the rest of the race was at the finish line. I saw it approaching and decided to give one last kick and so I gave it all I had. What a letdown it was when I crossed the line only to find that it wasn't the finish line at all and I still had another block to run!

I made it without walking and had run the race that I wanted to (except at the end when I had to whoop that 80 year old). I was so proud. It truly was the most athletic thing I had done in my life since my last college football game. It was a highlight for me. It was a HighFive moment and I was glad that I had entered the race.

Too often we miss our HighFive moments because we are running someone else's race. We start out on our own and doing what we think is right and then we begin to be influenced by those small little rear ends that are passing us by. It can be a neighbor that gets a nicer car or a fellow worker who cheats to get ahead, or something we see on TV that makes us want the "good life" sooner than we are prepared to handle it. Resist. Make sure you are in the race, but make it your race not your neighbors.

If you decide that your race is to come in first place and not just "place," you must prepare with that in mind. You must be aware of the sacrifices required in order to make it a race you own versus just your own race. In a race you own, you are preparing to compete and own everybody else's race. The bar is higher, the task is harder, but I am not sure that the reward is any greater than for the person who has established what the parameters of their race should be and they achieve it. I was as happy that I completed a half marathon without walking as the person who crossed the finish line first. Both were admirable goals. We were both in control of our own races.

HighFive Your Life Principle

Make sure you are in the race, but run your own race at your own pace.

CHAPTER 15

Preparation for Victory
Is Part of the Victory

Before anything else, preparation is the key to success.
—Alexander Graham Bell

Many months after the half marathon and after I had stopped my everyday running, I was still nagged by the thought that I should run a full marathon. I was also scared about not being able to finish it if I tried. It seemed like a big effort to go sign up and travel to participate in a marathon. I finally decided that I could create my own marathon by just running on a track at a local school.

I contacted the principal of a middle school by my house and made arrangements to use the track on an upcoming Saturday morning. I received permission to drive my RV down to the track so that I would at least have a bathroom.

The day came and I was on the track before daylight. I devised a system using two big bowls and 104 marbles. I placed all of the marbles in one bowl and set both bowls in chairs alongside the track. Each time I ran by, I would transfer one marble from the full bowl to the other bowl. I took a tape recorder and every now and then would record my thoughts. I was as ready as I could be for this great adventure, except in one very important aspect. I had not been training very hard for this at all. I ran often but also missed many days and didn't push myself as hard as I had in the past. I felt that there was no danger of me dying because my pace was so slow that if I really got tired, I could just stop running and start walking.

Daybreak found me jogging around the track . . . 10 laps then 20 laps . . . 30 then 40 slowly disappeared behind me. My friend who had run the half marathon showed up to encourage me. He walked alongside me as I continued on my run. As I got closer to 70 laps, the nature of my run took a turn for the worse. I began to labor to catch my breath and was getting light headed. As I finished my 70th lap, I stopped and walked off the track onto the grass.

If I thought that stopping the race was going to give me some relief, I was sorely mistaken. Suddenly my body just shut down. My face started going numb and I could not catch my breath. Other friends had just arrived to cheer me on only to find me in great agony on the side of the track. Someone wanted to call the ambulance and I said no. I lay down and then my calves began to cramp so badly that I had to stand up. We all started to get scared and so an ambulance was called. Soon seven para-medics were working on me complete with an IV and a ride to the hos-pital. At the hospital the tests were negative for a heart attack but showed that I may have had pneumonia. They kept me under observation. I finally threw up all of the power drinks I had been consuming and began to feel better. That night I was back at a church event where I had prom-ised to be the MC.

My wife and kids get a kick out of the experience they had as they heard the ambulances drive by our house on the way to pick me up. They never let me live it down. It was a funny experience except that it was so embarrassing, and I could have died. I am glad that friends were there to get me some help.

The HighFive Your Life principle is that preparation is key for any significant success that you seek, and that solid preparation for the victory is part of the victory. There generally are no short cuts to get there. Too often you desire what you see others in your circle do or have but are not willing to pay the price in preparation to achieve it. Like patience, the value in preparation occurs while you are doing it and not just when the desired result is reached. While you discipline yourself to the hard work of preparation, you are already reaping the value of that preparation. It does something good for the soul to be prepared. It gives you self confidence. It helps in your performance. It just feels good to be prepared and it is a great way to HighFive Your Life!

HighFive Your Life Principle

Preparation is key for any significant success that you seek, and solid preparation for the victory is part of the victory.

CHAPTER 16

The Oak Tree Lust

*You fall out of your mother's womb, you crawl across open country under
fire, and drop into your grave.*

—Quentin Crisp

When we moved to Lake Ola in Tangerine, Florida, I fell in love
with the property not the house. The house was a special place
built in 1932, but it was the trees, lake, and space outside that really
attracted me. We had many huge oak trees, but none were as big as the
three huge oaks on my neighbor's property. I found that as the years
went by, occasionally I would wish that I owned them. Given the other
things going on in my life, this covetous character flaw was only a minor
distraction. I was grateful for my beautiful five acres and all the beautiful
trees and bushes on them.

One day my neighbor, with whom we had a great relationship,
decided to put his house up for sale and move. We were not in a position
make an offer, but after some time of not selling, my neighbor and I
started negotiating and we purchased his 2.5 acres along with the house
that was on it. I hardly cared about the house. It was the trees that bedaz-
zled me. Particularly, there was one monster oak that was the crown
jewel.

A year or two later, as I was admiring that oak, I came to a sobering
and humbling realization. Even though I owned the property, I did not
own the trees. That monster oak was probably 200–300 years old and
had seen many things in its lifetime. I probably have 20–30 years left if
I am lucky and then I will be gone, and will have been just another

human to cross its path. I was not an owner; I was just a caretaker. I felt small and a little stupid to think that I had somehow thought I was bigger than that huge old oak.

My son Robbie with the big oak that caused me so much emotion!

The HighFive Your Life principle is that we are here on this earth for a short period of time and it is during that time that we need to take care of the important things and people around us. After that, we are gone and the earth just keeps right on turning—the birds keep chirping, the grass keeps growing, and only a few will notice that we have come and gone. It seems sad at first, but that is how it is, and if you think about it for a minute, you wouldn't have it any other way. It is our children's turn and then their children's turn. We need to leave this beautiful earth a little better than we found it. We need to teach our children to live a little better than we did. We need to do this while being proud of our efforts even if we don't live our lives perfectly.

When my father died in 2005, my mom had a headstone made and included her resting place at his side. I do not need to ponder what she might have been thinking when we visited the grave site recently and she stood before her own headstone. I did not need to wonder what her thoughts were because she had provided a space also for each of her children and their families so when I took this picture, I was standing in or around the spot where I will most likely be buried. Whether you are a person of faith or not, this life is the time to do your work, whatever that may be. There are many things that will tend to distract you, and you have to make a concerted effort to focus on the things that are most important. You can HighFive Your Life when you realize that there is no permanent earthly possession that you take with you forever. My big old oak is not mine at all. I am simply a caretaker, and there is peace in that knowledge.

HighFive Your Life Principle

We need to take care of the people and things that are important to us during our time here on this earth. We are caretakers not owners of our earthly possessions because we can't take them with us wherever we go 100 years from now.

Chapter 17

More Lessons from Oaks and Rivers

Almost every wise saying has an opposite one, no less wise, to balance it."
—George Santayana

One day during a particularly hard spring wind, we noticed that one of the big oaks had split and that with each gust of wind, the gap would open and close. We had to undertake a painful and expensive process of trimming back the huge limbs with the hopes that the tree would recover and produce new growth.

The tree expert came out and told us that the current practice for oaks like these is to trim them when they are small so that no low limbs are allowed to grow like the old ones in my yard. He said that if they are not trimmed when they are young, these trees will split when they are older.

The HighFive Your Life principle to consider is that as we raise our kids, coach our teams, or teach our classes, it is important to trim and trim and trim and help those with whom we have responsibility to grow straight and true. If we do not trim the branches that take off in a direction that experience has shown us will cause problems in the future, we are not showing the proper concern for the tree. If we allow certain behaviors in our youth that have been time tested to be detrimental in the long run, we likewise do not show the proper concern for our youth.

In that same wind storm, my neighbor on the other side of my house who owns a tree farm had many of his 15 foot tall oaks in pots blow over. We went next door to help stand them up and he pointed out that many of his oaks were really no good anymore because they had become root bound in their pots. They needed to be moved to bigger pots or planted in order to allow the roots to grow properly.

The HighFive Your Life principle to consider is that as we raise our kids or coach our teams or teach our classes, it is important to give them room to grow or they will not grow properly. If we smother our kids and do not allow them to have experiences where they can succeed or fail, we rob them of the opportunity to sink their roots deep. Our well intended efforts to protect them, at some point, begin to stunt their growth.

Author with his mother in front of the oak that split

It is interesting that as with most principles of life, there needs to be a balance. As parents, coaches, and teachers, we need to seek wisdom to know when to trim and when to let grow. Often times we don't get it right and need to adjust. Through our efforts to be patient, we will find a way. As with all things where patience is concerned, quitting is the only danger. We should not simply say "I am going to trim all the time" or "I am going to let them grow all the time." There is always a season and a balance that need to be considered.

I have tended to be a more conservative parent and have done a lot of trimming. My parents were probably good trimmers and growth promoters at the same time. I can't believe all of the things that they allowed me to do in terms of work and responsibility. As I have raised my children, the fear of something bad happening has sometimes kept my wife and me in a trimming mode too much.

When I was about 21 years old, I went to Utah to take some university classes during the summer. My brother-in-law was starting law school and was also in Utah with my sister. We decided we wanted to go down the Provo River in a kayak. We purchased an inflatable kayak at a local store along with helmets, paddles, and life vests. Neither of us had much experience with this and we were not really aware or concerned that the summer runoff in June made the river a roaring nightmare in certain spots.

There was a particularly fast part of the river at a place called Bridal Veil Falls. There were some buildings and improvements there, along with a walkway where spectators could view the river. We decided to start upriver a mile or so where it was a lot slower to try and get the feel for how to maneuver the kayak. I sat in back and my brother-in-law was in front.

We got the hang of it and thought we knew what we were doing by the time we reached Bridal Veil. As we approached it, I remember waving at people on the walkway. In retrospect, they must have thought we were crazy. We came around a bend and what had been adrenaline and excitement turned into fear. The water turned into roaring rapids and we were quickly out of our league. There were boulders everywhere and as hard as we paddled it felt like we are at the mercy of the river.

About halfway through we grabbed some tree branches and managed to pull our way out of the main stream and climb on to dry land. We were shaking and so glad that our lives had been spared. I'd had enough, though, and was ready to quit. Unfortunately, we soon found that we were on an island. We tried to wade across but there was just no way. We finally decided that as much as we did not want to get back in that kayak, there was no other way. We got in and soon were once again in the turbulent waters. We went over three small waterfalls and finally capsized near the bank and crawled out on to a path, relieved again to be alive.

I relate this story because the worse part of the whole thing was that in an effort to be what I thought was safe, I tied myself to the kayak with a rope. My thinking was that if we capsized, I wanted to be able to get back to the boat. Only later did I learn that I had actually created a death trap for myself.

I learned this lesson some six weeks later on the same river. By this time, we had purchased a six man raft and were trying to ferry some goods across the river for a camping trip. We had strung a rope across the river to ferry over our supplies. I was trying to hold the rope with my hands and keep my feet in the raft and move it along towards the other bank. As soon as we got into the fast water, however, I was flipped from the boat but did not let go of the rope. The raft was on top of me and I could not pull myself against the water. My only way out was to let go of the rope, which I did, and soon I bobbed up and swam to safety.

The rope that I had used in my very first adventure in the kayak on the river could have killed me if I had fallen out of the kayak and the rope had become caught on a rock with me on one side and the kayak on the other. I would never have been able to untie myself and never been able to swim against the current. What I thought was my lifeline was in actuality my deathline.

We need to make sure that what we think is a lifeline somehow does not create a drag to the point where instead of encouraging people to challenge life, we inadvertently make them afraid of it. I sometimes struggle to give those around me room to grow while still trying to trim where I need to. Recognizing this process and seeking wisdom for the correct balance to these two principles is a good way to HighFive Your Life and the lives of those around you.

HighFive Your Life Principle

We must always seek a balance between seemingly opposing life principles. Sometimes it is right to trim and other times it is right to let grow.

Chapter 18

Hey Dad, Water's Deep, Where's Jeep?

An Ounce of Prevention is Worth a Pound of Cure.

—*Ben Franklin*

Every few years, state officials would lower the water in Lake Tohopekaliga, located in Kissimmee, Florida, in order to expose the lake bottom and allow grasses to grow that removed the nutrients. It is a large lake about 9 miles long with locks at the south end. As the lake bottom began to be exposed, it became a great place for campfires, four-wheeling, and mudslinging for all of the locals.

Not all of the water would drain out, however, so there were various places where there were still water holes. I am not sure whose idea it was but my dad, my younger brother, and I decided that we should cross the lake bottom in our Jeep just to say that we had done it.

We started out from the west side on dry lake bottom but soon began to get into the water. It was only about 6 inches deep, but my dad thought that I should get out in front of the Jeep and walk just to make sure it didn't get too deep. I was only about 15, so that was not my idea of riding the Jeep across the lake bottom. My brother and I got out on the hood of the Jeep and I convinced Dad that I would get out and walk if the water got about a foot deep. We proceeded.

What we had not taken into account was that the channel for the boats getting to and from the marina was cut right through the path on which we were heading. We soon discovered that this channel did not have nice slowly slanted slopes, but was much more of a complete drop off.

All of a sudden the front of the Jeep disappeared. My brother and I scrambled towards the windshield where I could not help but see my father's face. I will never forget it—my father's face with water up across his chest in the driver's seat. We all climbed around to the back of the Jeep, which was still above water. People were stopping looking from the lake front at the whole spectacle. There we were, three sheepish men trudging back to shore to call the wrecker. By the time it arrived the Jeep had completely disappeared. I swam underwater with the hook and cable and we soon had it out.

The next day the headline in the local newspaper was "Hey Dad, Water's Deep, Where's Jeep?"

There are a couple of HighFive Your Life principles that we can glean from this experience. First, we laugh about it to this day. Other than our pride being hurt, there were no injuries. There were a few minor things we had to fix on the Jeep but it ran fine. It is a great fun memory for our family, and wasn't as bad as it may have seemed at the moment. Many things like that happen in our lives which seem so serious but later on simply become great fodder for Sunday afternoon family dinners when a good laugh is needed.

Second, I did not heed the call for some degree of prudence that my father had requested. That simple task alone would have prevented the whole episode. Think about how that principle of prudence or an ounce of caution or prevention could be applied to your life. Seatbelts are a great example.

Many years later on the way back to my house, traffic came to a standstill about a half mile from my driveway. I could tell that there was a wreck ahead somewhere and began to worry about who might have been coming to see me. As I got closer, it was apparent that it had occurred directly in front of my house. The officers allowed me to turn into my driveway and after parking my car, I returned to the scene. There had been a head on collision. In the car that got the worst of it were a mother and a young son, maybe 12 years old. They were on their way to church. The mother was flown to the hospital and died. The boy was just standing there with his shirt off in front of my house. He had a big red stripe across his chest where his seatbelt had marked him while saving his life. The mother had not been wearing one.

That simple precaution changed the whole landscape of his life and the lack of it ended the life of his mother. We should not live our lives in fear, but we should be prudent and cautious in the many things in our lives that take just a few extra seconds or just a little more effort to accomplish. That is a great way to HighFive Your Life.

HighFive Your Life Principle

Many tough events in our lives seem so serious, but over time become subjects of humorous family dinner conversations.

HighFive Your Life Principle

Sometimes with only a minimal amount of effort and caution we can avoid dangerous and unnecessary incidents.

CHAPTER 19

You Are What You Write . . . at Least to Your Great Grandchildren

Forgive, O Lord, my little jokes on Thee,
And I'll forgive Thy great big one on me.

—*Robert Frost*

Keeping a journal became important to me the first day of college. It may have been the excitement of it all or that I knew that I was entering into a new and special phase of life that I wanted to remember. Whatever it was, I have been fairly diligent about keeping one for the last 30 plus years. My first entry into my first real journal was on my first day of college.

> *Monday 9:00 P.M. September 8th, 1975*
> *I just left Mom and Dad at the car. We all hugged and cried and as they drove off, I felt so alone but also I felt a sense of excitement in the air. I came back and Benson, Chip, and I rearranged our room so that the beds are in the same room. It was kind of fun and neat to be on our own. I finally wrote my letter to Robbie and that took a load off my mind. I really miss her. I also wrote Joe and Calico. We met Carol, our RA, tonight. She seems like a real neat person. There are 19 guys and 0 girls in our coed dorm. The beds are so long and the sheets are so short. I met a few football players today and they look pretty good and big. Got a checking account.*

I have also enhanced my journal keeping with scrapbooks and photo albums, sometimes combining them into one. Presently, I have over 40 volumes of journals and many more scrapbooks and photo albums. I have an extracted wisdom tooth; bus, movie, and airplane tickets; multiple kinds of notes and letters; pictures, etc. Basically, I try and keep a record or history of my life. I try and write something for everyday on my computer while keeping the miscellaneous things in a file. Once a month I consolidate it and move it over into my journal.

My Journals

Several interesting observations can be made about journal keeping.

First, my wife argues that it is somewhat a waste of time and that I am burdening someone, presumably her and then the kids, with the responsibility to take care of them after I am gone. We laugh about it but there is some truth to it. It is a very valid question to ask who, besides me, even cares? I am one of billions of people that have lived and died. Who cares about my life?

The quick answer is that I care! However, it goes beyond that. I have enjoyed reading the histories of my ancestors to the extent that we have them. I am confident that 100 years from now, one of my great grandchildren is going to find my journals to be of great worth. Granted he or she might prefer a cool million in inheritance money, but I think this record will mean more to them. My journals allow me to reach forward to them and to share the kinds of things that I might have shared had I been sitting on a dock fishing or driving across the country with them. Somewhere in the boring day-to-day things that I write, I believe that someone will find something of importance many years from now.

Another interesting observation is that my journals contain my version of history. That is an important life lesson to learn. We see things through our own mind's eye and that is most often different than what the next person sees. Another of my wife's journal jokes is that she is going to rewrite them once I am gone so that they reflect the truth. I am sure that there is some truth in what she says. By writing however, especially for extended periods of time, it becomes clear that our journals are one-sided and we need to be aware in this life that there truly is always another side to the story.

The third observation that I would like to make is that I have been troubled by the thought that if someone ever does decide to read these 100 years from now, I will be defined by what they read. It makes me want to add disclaimers, which I do from time to time, to say, this does not contain the whole story. I really am a happy person. Nobody has the time, energy, or resources to write the whole story. My journal therefore is not only one-sided, it is incomplete and unable to convey the whole emotions of the day leading up to the event about which I might be writing at the time.

Despite those observations, keeping a journal is a great way to High-Five Your Life. It reminds you that you are worth writing about, even if it is only you that is doing the reading. It is a great vehicle for you to pass along life's lessons to those that are coming after you. There is inherent value in your story even if your life has been imperfect. In fact, the great value of your journals for your decedents is found in how you work your way through the trials of life and the comforting thought that even Grandpa had the same normal struggles as everyone else. Personal written words of your life and struggles that extend across generational gaps will be welcomed by future family members fortunate enough to read them.

A journal will help you HighFive Your Life because it will help remind you that your version of history is sometimes not complete and that there are other sides of the story. That realization all by itself might be enough to make you more tolerant and patient with others, which will go a long way towards bringing peace to your life.

HighFive Your Life Principle

Keeping a journal or diary will allow you to communicate with those in your family that are decades from being born. It is a reminder that you are worth writing about even if you are the only reader while you are alive.

Chapter 20

Ooops.... What Happened to My Investment?

Goodness is the only investment that never fails.
—Henry David Thoreau

When we first moved to our 24-acre farm in Apopka, Florida, I fulfilled a dream of mine and took the kids to a livestock auction and, as I recall, bought 18 cows. We built the fences to hold them on our property, but had none of the other necessary equipment to be able to control and move our cows properly. We just pulled up with the trailer and let them out into a small pasture.

When it was time to move them to a different pasture, there was no way to get them there except through our front yard. There was no guarantee that they would make it to the open gate leading into the other pasture on the other side of the yard. We decided to herd them up and put them back in our cow trailer and just haul them into the other pasture. We pulled the trailer into the pasture and opened the rear of it and began to try and get the cows to go up inside the trailer. It was actually a pretty comical scene to behold, and I apologize to my real cowboy friends for being such a greenhorn. My friend and I would get behind the cows waving PVC pipe in our hands and herd the cows towards the trailer. Of course, as the cows got closer to the trailer, they would veer off and not even come close to climbing in. The more we chased, the more anxious the cows got. Finally, one of them had enough and just jumped the fence like it was not even there. Off it went down our driveway and out onto the road. We jumped in the car and caught up with it near a public schoo,l but it then disappeared into a forest behind the school. That was that; my cow was just gone and I had few options to get it back.

One evening, about a week later, I was sitting on our front patio speaking with my father-in-law when we saw a police car with lights flashing moving slowly along the road by our front pasture. It was dark, but we could make out a set of legs moving along in front of his car in his headlights. It gradually dawned on me that this could be my cow so I ran to open a gate. The cow actually turned down our long driveway and headed for us until it caught our scent or recognized our place from the week before. It suddenly turned on a dime and sprinted right towards the police officer that had trailed it down our driveway. It ran by the police car and just like that, we were back on the road trying to chase it down. This time we had help chasing it and the word eventually came that they had it cornered in a neighborhood about two miles from my home.

We got there and sure enough, there it was in a residential lot with a wall behind it. There were several officers of the law with us now, but still we had no viable way to get it. Thank goodness there is an agricultural unit with the sheriff's department that specializes in these types of incidents and he was on his way. Apparently the gun that shoots the darts to put it asleep was being used elsewhere so he showed up with a horse trailer and three lariats. He asked me if I could use one and of course I had to say yes. The three of us approached the cow slowly with onlookers taking in the whole spectacle. It lasted about one minute. We spread out and inched closer and the cow finally decided that he was done with us and just ran by us and disappeared, this time for good. I never saw him again.

On another occasion, my brother and I made a lowball offer on a really run-down home. We had a few rental properties and were looking for another. Being the astute investors that we were, we offered about half of what the seller was asking and were surprised but pretty excited when it was accepted. It was not a few days after the closing, however, that we got a notice that the house had been condemned and needed to be torn down! We could not believe it. Our real estate agent was our friend and we decided not to pursue any recourse. Not only did we not have a house to rent, we had to pay to tear it down and have it removed. These two stories are just a couple of examples from many where I have made an oops in my investments.

Nobody likes to lose money on an investment, but sometimes you just do. As painful as it may be, the very act of investing money carries with it an inherent risk. If you own something there is always a risk that it may disappear one day. Sometimes it is within your control and sometimes it is outside your control. Sometimes that is just the way it is. You can HighFive Your Life by being smart with your money. You can HighFive Your Life by learning from your financial mistakes and being a better steward over your assets. You can also HighFive Your Life by knowing that you may lose something along the way despite your best efforts. Clearly your efforts will be better than my efforts in the two examples I shared. However, you may still lose. You can recover. There are so many things more important than your money. Your life has so much more to offer than the accumulation of assets. Work hard to achieve your financial goals, but you can HighFive Your Life by keeping your assets in the proper perspective.

HighFive Your Life Principle

Learn from your financial mistakes and be a better steward over your assets, but always remember that they are not the purpose of your life.

CHAPTER 21

Just How Important Is Money?

Money often costs too much.

—Ralph Waldo Emerson

Well, the answer to that question seems pretty simple if you are short on your house payment. Money is the medium we use to trade our labor, intelligence, luck, determination, good fortune, and skills for what we want to possess. It is spoken of in both positive and negative ways. It motivates people to make both right and wrong choices. It is used by many as a measure of life's success—to keep the score on life's up and down journey. It is part of our everyday life in some form or fashion, whether we like it or not. So, I ask again, just how important is money?

My wife taught me a great lesson that may seem trivial at first, but in actuality gets to the heart of the answer to the question I have posed. Before I married Joey, I had been seeking to get married for several years. It was something that I had looked forward to for as long as I can remember. As time went by I wondered if I would ever find the right person for me. I dated many wonderful ladies but never found the right match.

To help me hold on to the hope of one day finding her, I began to keep my pocket change in a big jar. I would throw in some cold hard cash every now and then for good measure. I also added an occasional note with a thought about my future wife. Sometimes I would write directly to her. The note would fall to the level of the money and soon be buried by more coins and cash. I determined that when I found the right lady, this would be my gift to her. Years went by and the jars began to increase. By the time I got engaged at the age of 31, I had accumulated quite a treasure.

The night came, just a day or two before our wedding, that I presented Joey with the gift. I told her what I had done and invited her to begin to open the jars. To my surprise, the money had no significance to her. It was actually a lot of work to get the contents of the bottles out and as she worked at it she struggled to get through the money so that she could find the note. A fifty or a hundred dollar bill meant little to her as she brushed by them to get to a note. When she found a note there would be a pause as she read it and then she laughed or sighed. It really was one of the most romantic things I have ever done and it really put into contrast the value of money with the value of love.

Of course she was grateful for the money. We both had jobs and had been working, but now that we would be married we had to be much more careful with our spending. It turned out there was about $5000 in those jars, but the real treasure that night to Joey was in those scribbled notes written by a man who longed to find the woman of his dreams and finally did.

You can HighFiveYour Life by simply reminding yourself from time to time that the Holy Grail of Life is not found in money but in real heartfelt love for another person. We go through life using money to help us achieve many of our wants and needs, but the true love of another person is a want and need which cannot be bought or traded with money. Look around you. There is treasure close by. HighFive Your Life by recognizing those people that are special in your life and share your love with them.

HighFive Your Life Principle

Remind yourself from time to time that the Holy Grail of Life is not found in money, but in the real heartfelt love for another person.

Should Have Thought of that Leak Thing Before Launching

We are born wet, naked, and hungry. Then things get worse.
—*Author Unknown*

When I was a senior in high school, I somehow got it into my head that I wanted to build a houseboat. It started with the thought of getting four 55 gallon drums and jury-rigging them together with some 2x4s, adding a platform, and then just floating in the lake. The idea grew, however, and I was soon scouring the junkyard for what ended up being six 55 gallon drums on each side of a several thousand pound monstrosity, of which I was very proud.

My father had a shop where he serviced all of his trucks and equipment and had a mechanic that took care of them. His name was Bill, and he could fix anything that ever came through those doors. He and my dad taught me to weld and use the torch and a few other useful mechanical skills. As the project grew, we decided that it needed to be built outside on a platform of blocks so that when we did decide to take it to a lake (if we ever got that far) we could back a lowboy trailer underneath it. I'm sure my dad thought of that, as I don't think I ever thought that far ahead.

Over the course of the next several months after school and on weekends, I would go out with my buddy and partner Jimmy to work on the boat. I learned how to fiberglass and do electrical wiring and siding and quite a few other basic carpentry skills. This boat had a captain's steering wheel, a carpeted ceiling, a generator-powered lighting system, and a deck on the roof that was sturdy enough to take everyone upstairs for a ~~pain dive (a dive that really shows your friends just how much pain you~~ can take) into the lake.

It was a beautiful sight to see as it gradually came together. I am sure that in retrospect, my mom and dad were glad to have me involved in something that challenged me and kept me busy. I could make a lot of mistakes and not really hurt anyone. I did make one big mistake, however. I began to realize as I estimated the weight of the building on top of the twelve 55 gallon drums that my beautiful boat was not going to float. It was just too heavy and needed more buoyancy. I made yet another trip to the junk yard and found a 230 gallon airplane wing tank.

I calculated that if I could get it totally submerged, it would keep the boat afloat. I am not sure how much dad and Bill helped us design and build an attachment for the tank to hook to the underbelly of the houseboat, but I am sure we must have had a lot of assistance.

As school came to a close, we were ready to launch the boat and I christened her *Fresca,* after the beverage. I did not drink alcohol and generally used Fresca as my cool substitute when I went to parties. I even painted her green and white to match the Fresca can colors. When I think back at what it took to build the boat and then to haul it to the lake and launch it, I am forever grateful to my dad. Where else could a young teenager have access to a bulldozer and a mechanic to make a dream become a reality? Soon Dad was on the bulldozer clearing out a place for the trailer to back under the boat. It was time to take *Fresca* to the lake for her maiden voyage.

We must have been a sight as we went down the road heading to the dock at Lake Tohopakeliga in Kissimmee, Florida.

The hyacinths were clogging the dock area but they were no match for the big hefty houseboat and the lowboy that hauled it.

Little by little, we backed down the ramp, not knowing exactly what to expect.

At the appropriate time (when we didn't sink), I broke a big bottle of *Fresca* to christen her (that is actually harder to do than it seems).

We managed to drive her across the lake where a good family friend allowed us to use their canal to park the boat. The canal was also filled with hyacinths, but we managed to sling them out of the way and get *Fresca* safely to harbor.

Mr. Northrop, author, David, Randy, Carlos, Bill, and Fred

We spent the next couple of weeks putting some finishing touches on the boat, but noticed that she was not riding as high out of the water as when we launched her. If you went to a corner of the boat, that corner would almost go under water. I soon discovered that the airplane tank that was supposed to be giving me extra lift had filled up with water. Apparently, I had not done a very good job of fiberglassing all of the holes in it.

Now the big job was to get in the water, unhook the tank and get it back to the shop to undergo repairs. We unhooked it okay, but it was so heavy that as soon as it came unhooked, it fell to the bottom of the lake and then rolled to the deepest hole in the canal. Not to worry, though. My friend Fred ran home and got some scuba gear and found it for us and we were able to hook it to my Jeep with a rope and pull it up to the shore.

After a good fiberglassing and checking and rechecking, it was time to return it to the bottom of the boat. The problem was that we had a 230 gallon buoy that was impossible to push under water. We figured out that we needed to fill it back up with water to get it to go under water enough so that we could get it under the boat. With some hesitation, I drilled a hole in the top of it and filled it almost full with water and reattached it to the boat. Next, we drilled a hole in the floor of the boat and ran a pipe with a pump on the top of it down into the tank. Then using a drill to make the pump turn, we pumped the tank dry and patched the hole. The problem was solved!

We spent the next two months spending the night on the lake and fishing and just having fun. Then it was time to go to college. My parents did not want to impose any further on our neighbors and so insisted that we pull it back out of the water. It was a massive effort with the lowboy and bulldozer, but we got it out. It was parked in our backyard for years where it gradually rotted away, until one day it was hauled off. It was a short lived project but a great learning one for me and my friends!

Author's father and mother taking Fresca on a test run

What does this story have to do with your ability and duty to High-Five Your life?

There are actually some very real life lessons in this houseboat that I only realized much later in my life, and they center on the ability to understand how to buoy yourself up when the burdens of life seem too heavy.

Some of the biggest burdens of life come when we regret some action that we have done but shouldn't have, or should have done but didn't. In a spiritual sense, we would call these sins. We fret over them and have remorse over them, as well we should. We each try to do what is right, whether it is spiritually based or morally based or both. When we are less than what we know we should be, we feel down and disappointed.

Let me address this problem from both a spiritual and moral perspective. This sensation, this Godly sorrow or awareness in our consciousness, is meant to drive us towards repentance. Repentance is the act of turning away from or discontinuing the sinful action. In this sense, Godly sorrow benefits society and the individual. From a purely moral sense, it pains your conscience and you have a desire to correct your action. You may need to return something that was stolen, offer an apology, or stop a particular behavior. Inside you know that it is something that needs to change.

This is a positive thing for you and society, whether it is Godly sorrow or a strong moral conscience or both. The problem comes when our Godly sorrow or our conscience decide to remain remorseful even after you have taken the necessary steps to repent or correct your behavior. At that point, we sometimes move from a healthy desire to improve into a depressed state of "I'm no good," or "I am a lousy person." We begin to wallow in our weaknesses and the world begins to look more sullen and gray. Gone are the bright days of spring in our minds. We just continually stay in the state of "I am just not good enough."

This is an outright deception and incorrect self assessment. In the houseboat story, I found out that my boat was too heavy and I found a solution to solve that problem, which was the additional wing tank that I added. It was a good solution but when it began to fill up with water instead of providing buoyancy, it created more weight and was actually a drag to the boat. Once I fixed the leaks in it and returned it to the boat, it did its job perfectly.

In life, our conscience or Godly sorrow is a mechanism to lift our burdens by helping us return to doing what is right and abandon the course of action that we know to be wrong. In Christianity, Jesus is the source of lifting and curing and carrying our burdens for us as we repent and are forgiven. This process of removing burdens is a gift from God. However, when Godly sorrow or our conscience begins to drive us beyond this mark, what was once a very good thing becomes a counterfeit. If we cannot forgive ourselves and do not accept the gift of forgiveness, we frustrate the plan of happiness. Then we become as the added tank on the houseboat that filled with water; this God-given gift of sorrow, instead of lifting us, becomes a burden and drag because it sends an unhealthy and wrong message that we are somehow less deserving or worthy of a wonderful life. Once you have corrected your life, forgive yourself. Let your life be buoyed up by this act of forgiveness.

The process of repentance is meant to make you lighter after a time of sorrow and remorse. We are all imperfect beings and yet we are designed for joy and happiness and peace of mind. Use the tool or gift of Godly sorrow to make corrections in your life and then move on.

HighFive Your Life Principle

Use the blessing of your conscious to change your behavior. Once you have corrected the mistake, do not allow yourself to dwell in sorrow. Forgive yourself and move on.

CHAPTER 23

Learn from the Broken Down Barn

Here is the test to find whether your mission on earth is finished. If you're alive, it isn't.

—*Richard Bach*

In 2005 when we sold our business, we bought a 535-acre old dairy farm near Antigo, Wisconsin for hunting and recreational purposes. It had long since shut down as a dairy, but was rich in history. One of the unique things that this farm offered was the purported largest hip barn in the whole state of Wisconsin. It is huge!

When the barn was built in 1912, it was the accomplishment of someone with a lot of vision. It served a very important purpose as both a place to milk the cows in the bottom story and to store hay and feed in the level above. You can imagine the pride of the owner and the workers that put together such a magnificent structure. It served its purpose well day after day, decade after decade. Often it was beset by raging wind and snow storms but withstood them proudly. Over the years one would assume that repairs were made to keep the structure intact and able to accomplish its purpose.

And then the inevitable happened as the farm changed hands and the dairy ceased operating. It became a cattle farm and much of the dairy equipment was no longer needed. As time marched on and the farm changed hands yet again, the cattle operation ceased entirely. The new owner purchased the property to harvest the timber, and then we bought it for hunting and recreation.

That proud old barn that had stood for almost a century was now in our care. Even though we marvel at the structure and it is the attraction that everyone must see when they visit, the reality is that we have had no purpose for it. As time has passed and the storms have continued to rage, the barn has begun to break apart.

It is hard to watch but our funds are very limited. We invested money into repairing the home that is there, but have allocated little money for the barn. We recently spent a small amount to repair the roof and get a few more years out of it, but we did it only because we could not stand to see it fall to the ground.

The message is clear. Even proud structures, when they lose their purpose, begin to decay and slowly drift away. You see broken down barns all across the landscape of America. You also see broken down people everywhere.

As soon as a person loses their purpose, everything—their will to live, to challenge life, to properly maintain their bodies and minds, etc.—goes by the wayside. As we go through life, through marriage, through our careers, there will be times when we sense that our usefulness decreases. Of course this is not true, but to us in the moment it seems very real. Our boards and tin start to come off and nobody seems to care. Our walls start to lean and nobody comes to prop them up. Once strong and proud, now with the passage of time and with no purpose we are numbered among the others that the world seems to have passed by unnoticed and considered unimportant.

The HighFive Your Life principle is simply to never let that happen. There are different seasons in our lives to be sure. One day we are the star baseball player and the next day we are just one of the old guys hanging around the park. One day we are parents running our kids around everywhere, managing a household and all that entails and going to bed exhausted each night with the heavy anticipation of the next day being just the same. The next day, we are empty nesters with no children to haul around, no phone calls to arrange parties, no important counsel to give. One day we are going to work making a difference in our jobs; our coworkers respect us; our input is needed. We are proud of our work product. We earn money to support our family. The next day we are retired or out of a job and no longer are we proud of the results of our efforts at work.

These feelings of no purpose can be very real, but we should not let them be true. Changes are inevitable. Adjustments need to be made, but the one constant that we need to have is a sense of purpose. There are countless charities and organizations that are doing good deeds all over the world. There are books to write, new skills and hobbies to develop. If you are young and still in need of employment, you need to take charge of your life and make the necessary adjustments to start climbing back out. You need to find your purpose in self improvement. It is disappointing to me when someone says they will not take a job because it does not pay enough or they are worth far more. Money is not the issue. Work is very empowering all by itself and does much more for the soul than waiting on the sidelines for the perfect job. Whatever your talent, you will be happier if you take a job that provides some income while you plot and plan your next move. In most cases that will be better than just waiting for the perfect job to come. The value of your work product is not in your wage but in your effort. When a person is actively engaged, his thought process begins to see other opportunities that he may have missed while "waiting" for that perfect job.

In all aspects of life, we need to find our purpose and we need to allow that purpose to mature or change as the circumstances of our life change. Your life truly is worth a HighFive and should never become like the old barn.

HighFive Your Life Principle

Never, ever, ever lose your purpose in life. If you do not have one, find one.

CHAPTER 24

Don't Take My Fries Mister

If there is any one secret of success, it lies in the ability to get the other person's point of view and see things from that person's angle as well as from your own.

—*Henry Ford*

My trip to McDonalds on this day was a little different than most. I had never seen one so crowded, and I had to actually share a table with a man that was already occupying it. He was reading the paper and graciously allowed me to join him. After I got settled down, I reached over and took some of my fries. I was startled when shortly thereafter, he reached over and took some of my fries. It got very awkward very quickly. Not to lose out on any more of my fries, I reached over and grabbed some more. I couldn't believe it when he took more again. Finally he got up and left. Much to my chagrin, when he left he took the paper with him and under the paper, hidden from view, were my fries. The whole time I had been eating his fries! I was lucky that this guy didn't knock my head off.

It is very easy for us to begin to draw conclusions based on our point of view that have little or no relationship to reality. It happens around us all the time, but it just needs to happen to us personally once or twice and then we should learn this valuable lesson.

On another occasion I attended a hearing of some sort with our restaurant manager and an employee who no longer worked for us. The mission of the judge (if that is what he was) was to decide whether this employee was eligible for unemployment compensation. Our restaurant manager's position was that the employee was a no-call, no-show for several days and so he assumed she quit and took her off the schedule. The employee's position was that she did not quit but was fired, and therefore eligible for compensation.

The judge put both people under oath and I sat back and watched the proceedings. It has been a long time since this happened and I do not remember the outcome, but I can distinctly remember being amazed at how both people under oath told two different stories in which they each sincerely believed. I could see why people say things that seem so out of place to me. We may be experiencing the same event with other people and yet everyone is having a different experience.

There truly are at least two sides to every story, and you HighFive Your Life when you pause and seek to understand them before acting. It is within the realm of possibilities that you can actually be wrong! Becoming wise has at least part of its roots buried deep in this principle.

HighFive Your Life Principle

It is possible that your point of view is not correct, or only partly so. Slow down and seek to see all sides before acting. This is not a reason to not act, just a caution to base your actions on real data.

CHAPTER 25

Faith Hope and Love—It's Worth the Fight

In all things it is better to hope than to despair.
—Johann Wolfgang von Goethe

One day while serving a church mission, I was walking along a dusty road in Antofagasta, Chile. My missionary companion and I noticed an old lady sobbing on the side of the road. She was drunk and people were passing her by, paying no attention to her at all. We felt compassion and sat down and started talking with her. There was not a whole lot we could do, but my heart ached and ached for her. The thought went through my head that if she keeled over dead at that moment, probably nobody in the world would care. It hit me like a ton of bricks that the single most devastating thing that could happen to anybody is to think that nobody cares about them. To be devoid of love from anybody, to have no hope for the future, to have no faith that things will work out okay in the end—that is the antithesis of HighFive Your Life and a very lonely and desolate place.

I contemplated my own grandmother who was back in Florida. She was old and disabled, but the recipient of a tremendous amount of love and affection from all of her family. She was constantly getting visits, cards in the mail, and phone calls and knew without a doubt that she was loved. Having lost her husband some years earlier and being afflicted by a very debilitating case of rheumatoid arthritis, she had reasons to be sad and despondent. However, she overcame those very real life tragedies to find peace and happiness. I believe that was because she had faith, hope, and love.

My sister Danette had the foresight to give her a tape recorder before she passed away and asked her to talk about her life. Later, Danette transcribed the recording and had it printed and bound. My grandmother signed and dedicated one for each of her 9 grandchildren. Today it is one of the most important books in my possession. My kids know more about her than I ever could have shared, and it provides me with comfort and perspective that has been helpful in my later years. I wish everybody had a journal of the lives of their ancestors. That is an important reason why we each should keep our own history to pass along. There is power and good that can come from it.

My grandmother related the many funny experiences that she had growing up from pulling pranks on her sisters to setting the outhouse on fire. She talked about the many principles that her parents taught her such as to not buy on credit and to care for those in need. I love all of the stories in her book, but I have chosen a special section of it from which to take a few excerpts to express the attitude that Leah Futch Dossey had despite the circumstances of her life.

> *I live from one day to another, getting all out of life each day that I can possibly get. My dear loveable husband, after I took arthritis, waited on me as long as he was able, which was for quite some time. Then he became ill and was no longer able to care for me. He passed away on April 28, 1974. He has been gone 6 years and I have been alone. It has not been easy living without him. He was a wonderful husband and father. He taught his children many things. They constantly repeat "Daddy taught us that. It sounds so good to hear them honor their father so highly and I know it is true. We had a wonderful life together. No one could have had a better one. We worked hard but we loved hard. It was worth it all. I would not call him back into this wicked world if I could. Whatever happened, in my mind, it is for the best. That's God's will or it wouldn't be. He has watched over me, guided me, taken care of me, and he has led me. He has reconciled me to the life without my husband. I have seen Jackson quite often in my dreams. He most always kisses me in my dreams. I dreamed of him last night, so to me his spirit is with me, it is in this house. I feel him, I know he's here and I know*

that God is near. God is by my side always, he has never forsaken me. I believe that so truly. I believe that is the reason I have been so reconciled to give up a loved one. It has not been easy, but it has been made easier by God and God alone.

If you do not have God to believe in, have faith in, look to, depend on, you have nothing. No one no matter how much you love them and how much they do for you, can take the place of God or give you the comfort that comes within your heart and in your soul, but God and God alone. He is who I look to from day to day.

A few pages later after speaking of her sister's arthritis that left her a complete invalid, she relates:

I also have that same arthritis, I am afraid that I will not bear it as bravely as she did but I try and with God's help I get by. I am not an invalid, but I have had surgery on both hips, I have two steel hips, one steel and plastic knee, and one implant eye. I am just about made over, but it helps to have this done. It takes much of the pain away. This is my cross to bear. That is what my sister said and she bore it so bravely. I wish that I could bear it so bravely. I wish that I could bear it so bravely as she, and always be so faithful as she. But I complain more than she did but God's will I shall keep going as well as I am and I have many blessings. I have much to see and life is beautiful if you will try and find it. You can always find some good in anything or anybody if you will look for it. Speak not evil but try to find the good instead of the bad.

We have a beautiful world, many beautiful things to see if we have the time to look around us and see the beautiful things and the beautiful life and the beautiful country that God has provided us with.

This attitude is so different from that of the lady that I tried to comfort in Chile. The horrible misconception that would make someone feel so hopeless and without love makes each of us want to fight for her. It makes you mad. In the Bible the Apostle Paul encourages us to "Fight the good fight of faith." Is there such thing as a "good" fight? We know for sure that there is such a thing as a bad fight.

Attitude and Perseverance

I have had surgery on both hips, I have two steel hips, one steel and plastic knee, and one implant eye. I am just about made over. This is my cross to bear. This is what my sister said and she bore it bravely. I wish that I could bear it as bravely as she and always be as faithful as she. But I complain more than she did but God's will I shall keep going as well as I am. I have many blessings...many blessings every day. We have a beautiful world, many beautiful things to see if we have to the time to look around us and see the beautiful life and the beautiful country that God has provided us with.

Leah Futch Dossey 1908 – 1982 (Grandma)

Leah Futch Dossey

One day I was driving to the movie theater with my wife and infant son. We were just talking about the day as we went over a set of railroad tracks in our small town of Kissimmee. Suddenly the truck in front of me swerved off to the right into a parking lot and the driver started making clear gestures that he was mad at me. I did a stupid thing and pulled off the road, too, and walked straight back to him. He was ranting and raving about me being too close and tailgating him. I told him that my wife and little baby boy and I were on the way to the movies and had no idea what he was talking about. He settled a little and apologized. What a stupid move on my part. I was lucky.

Some years before, I heard of a situation where allegedly a young man and his girlfriend recklessly pulled out on a two lane highway in front of an older man driving his truck. According to what I heard, the older man was angry that he had done this and began to tailgate him around town until they pulled up to a stoplight at which point the young man got out of his car and headed back towards the truck. The older man felt threatened and pulled out a gun and shot him dead right there on the road. The sadness that this event caused and the lives that were changed helps me define this as a bad fight and makes me feel lucky that I didn't have a similar result when I got out of my car.

We know there are bad fights, but are there good ones? I can think of no better fight than the fight of faith, of hope for a better day, and of love for one another. When a person loses this trilogy of strength, the absolute depression, loneliness, and ugly gnawing at one's self worth make the fighting of this fight not only a "good" fight, but perhaps the most noble in all humanity.

As I got on the airplane to return home to my family after my two year mission in Chile, you can imagine the many thoughts running through my head. I had not been home or seen my parents in two years, and I was anxious to see them. I would be starting my graduate school in two weeks to begin the MBA program. Amidst all of the feelings and emotions that I was experiencing as I sat on that plane and prepared to leave Santiago, the most poignant one that I recall, was a very strong realization and commitment. I felt peace. I felt the peace that comes from service to others. For two years, I had been focused on others. I did not have any other distractions. The people of Chile were my life and I had given myself to them completely. It was then and there on that plane that I resolved as a 24-year-old young man, if I got to be fifty years old and owned twenty hotels (my family was in the hotel business back in Florida at that time), but did not have the feeling that I had at that moment, I would consider my life to be a failure.

I have often considered that very tough metric as I have evaluated my life. I know that the good feeling that I had comes from service to others, which is not natural to me. I am selfish and all too often worry about my own circumstances. In many cases, I have fallen way short of my goal. At the age of 55, it may be that this book and the whole High-Five Your Life theme is in some way an effort on my part to do a better job. I know that you can HighFive Your Life by fighting the good fight of having and sharing faith, hope, and love.

HighFive Your Life Principle

Faith, hope, and love are perhaps the greatest principles of life and worthy of our best fight.

CHAPTER 26

A Fight Worth Fighting
Is a Fight Worth Winning

I have not yet begun to fight!

—*John Paul Jones*

If in fact the challenge to rid the world of the feeling of despair that comes from the lack of faith, hope, and love, is a good and noble fight as discussed in the previous chapter, how should we fight it? I learned a lot from a good friend and powerful boxer named Ross Puritty.

The boxer story actually begins before I met Ross. A member of my staff at Water Mania was a very dedicated and hardworking person who was raising four children on her own. The father was in prison but was getting out soon. In an effort to help get some normalcy back into her home, I offered to help this man go to school or to get a fresh start in something. When she discussed this with him, he indicated that what he really wanted to do was box.

I was totally unfamiliar with how to get started with this idea, so I went to the phone book and started looking for a trainer. I finally found a trainer and he agreed to meet with us. At the meeting we agreed on a training price and a workout schedule to give this man the best shot at being a successful boxer. The short story is that it did not work out for various reasons, and several months later we stopped.

That could have been the end of the story, but a year or two later I got a phone call from that trainer with an interesting proposal. There was a heavyweight boxer named Ross Puritty that had just fought Tommy Morrison to a draw, had a 7–7 record, and was looking for a manager/sponsor to take him to the next level. My brother Randy and I were really intrigued with the idea. A heavyweight boxer! We were already past playing in the local softball leagues, which is where all of the frustrated athletes including us normally end up. Now with young children and busy jobs we just didn't have time. A heavyweight boxer touched somehow on our competitive spirit, and we decided to discuss it more.

I should have known that I was over my head when a guy nicknamed "Mouse" flew down to Florida to negotiate the contract. We put together a deal that paid Ross a certain amount to sign and a percentage of the winnings. The trainer and his wife came on board for a certain fee that included a percentage of the winnings. Randy and I got the balance of the winnings and basically all of the expenses.

We were very impressed with Ross. He was a good-looking man with a degree from University of Texas at El Paso, where he had played foot-ball. He was as sharp as a tack and built like a tank.

The Author, Randy, and Ross

Randy and I, being in the hotel business, provided room and board, a car for transportation, and also moral support. The trainer's responsibility was to train Ross and get fights, and Ross's responsibility was to train hard and win. The goal was to get his record improved to a point where he could get his million dollar fight with one of the big name fighters at that time. And so began a very up and down two years that had a lot of high moments and a lot of low moments.

Without telling the whole story, over time everyone became frustrated with everyone else. I soon found that nobody at the lower levels really wanted to fight Ross because he was strong and had an incredible knockout punch. We had to travel all over the southeast to get a fight. We had to not only pay for the expenses of the trip but generally for the other fighter to get in the ring with Ross. Each weekend that I had to tell my wife that I needed the family van for a boxing road trip created friction at home. Ross was frustrated that he was not getting the big fight. Some friction was developing between him and the trainer. The trainer was frustrated with Ross. Everyone was probably frustrated with Randy and me as we were not qualified to be a good manager for an aspiring heavyweight boxer.

At some point we even decided to host the first boxing match in Kissimmee's new civic center in an effort to build his record. We used the staff from Water Mania and sold tables to sponsors and put on quite an event. We lost a lot of money but Ross won his match and the fights were a fun event for the community.

After that event, however, tensions got too high and things unraveled. We all parted ways and began to try and undo our deal. Some time went by and the trainer was approached with what would be our biggest fight. There was a Fight Night program on TV and they were featuring an up-and-coming new heavyweight fighter and they needed a solid opponent. In the minds of the up-and-coming fighter's camp, they wanted a fighter that had some history and name recognition, but not someone that would beat their champ. In our camp, we saw this as an opportunity to get Ross on TV before a national audience and reintroduce him as a heavyweight contender. I believe that by this time, our "Team Puritty" had built his record to 17 wins and 7 losses. This was our last chance to take it to the next level and we all decided to overcome our frustrations and acrimony and get back together and go for it.

It was a unique experience for me. I found myself in Rochester, New York, walking around the back rooms of the event center trying to negotiate for a cut man (the guy in the corner who basically tries to stop the bleeding and swelling of the fighter during the fight). There were TV cameras, a weigh in, and all the other things you could imagine at a boxing match. In the locker room prior to the fight, I tried to find words of encouragement but it was mostly quiet. This was a different kind of competition than I was used to. I have played many college football games in front of thousands of fans but Ross was preparing for a battle where he was alone in the ring with a guy that wanted to take his head off. I don't remember what I said to Ross in that locker room before the fight, but I am quite sure that it wasn't very inspiring. What we all knew was that we had all been on a long journey and spent a lot of time, energy, and money to get here, and it was all riding on this match.

Much later in life I spoke with Ross about this fight and he confided that he went into the fight alone without feeling any support. The natural consequence of our Team Puritty's discord had a much deeper impact on him than I had previously considered. Each of us had our own disillusionments with our arrangement but only one of us had to actually go into the ring with that baggage and fight. In retrospect, probably the best thing I could have said to Ross in that locker room prior to the fight was simply that I believed in him.

When the fight started the energy level was intense. The opponent was big and strong, too. I am so glad that I was not in the ring. In the third round Ross took a hard hit to the head that staggered him. Much of the rest of the fight was a defensive battle for Ross. I watched the fight with the trainer's wife ringside and asked her if he was letting him know that he was losing. It was obvious to everyone that he was losing and I wanted to make sure that he knew that so that he could change his fight from being defensive to being offensive. She assured me that he was being told.

When the final bell rung and they raised the hand of the opponent as the winner in the decision, I could see from Ross's expression that he didn't agree with the decision. My brother and I were devastated with the loss. All of the distractions that this boxing adventure had caused in my and my brother's small families over the last two years, the financial investment, the stress in the relationships between manager/owner/trainer/fighter—all had taken a toll. However, it could have been mitigated to some degree by a victory in front of a national audience. Instead with the defeat, we all knew that this team was coming to an end.

As I joined Ross in that quiet and awkward locker room after the fight, I asked Ross if he knew that he was losing. He said that he did not know if he was winning, but did not think that he was losing. He said that he wasn't even tired, which of course was not what I wanted to hear. There was not much left to say. We agreed that we would meet in a few days back at the water park to go over the film and discuss it more then.

A few days later back in Florida, we watched the film in my office. Ross could not believe it. He could see finally what we had all seen watching the fight. It was not his best effort. He wanted a rematch much like I wanted to redo my Princeton football experience when I did not believe in myself enough to perform well, but it was not to be.

We all parted ways after that fight. Ross went on to a great career which ended with 31 wins and 20 losses, with 27 wins coming by knockouts. We had each learned a lot from that experience and were better for it. We each left with our own perspective about what had happened during those two years. I am certain that I was not a good boxing manager. I probably learned the most from that last fight, however, regarding HighFive Your Life principles. Soon after the fight I actually wrote down several things that I believe are useful to each of us as we fight the noble fight of faith, hope, and love. In the next several chapters I will share those with you.

HighFive Your Life Principle

In a fight there are winners and losers. It always feels better to be on the winning side if you have won fair and square. Make the maximum effort to win. This applies most importantly to fights regarding principles and values.

CHAPTER 27

Am I Winning?

(Lesson One from Chapter 26)

A winner never stops trying.

—*Tom Landry*

Sometimes we just don't know where we stand in the game of life. We are not sure if we are winning; we may just think that we are not losing. We wander from day to day, doing the things that are before us, things that require our attention, things that are a crisis, things that are mundane. We get up. We go to work. We come home. We go to bed. Then one day we wake up and we are fifty and we wonder what we have done with our life. Getting caught up in things that have no real importance to anything worthwhile is a place where many of us find ourselves, if we never force ourselves to answer that question: am I winning?

In order to win, you need to know what you are fighting for and understand what you are willing to expend to have victory. When you lose that vision, you also tend to lose the need to answer that question: am I winning? If you ask it truthfully, you will most likely find that the answer to that question, directly or indirectly, involves your relationships with other people. It may be your children or your spouse or the homeless or your employees. It may be the future recipients of a new drug that you are laboring to discover to cure a horrible disease. It may include personal goals like weight and health, but even those are blessings to those around you. Are you at peace with your effort? Are you winning? You can HighFive Your life by asking and answering those questions regularly and honestly, and then with that knowledge get back in the fight.

HighFive Your Life Principle

Evaluate often if you are winning or losing the fight in which you are engaged. Only with the knowledge of that truth can you plan well your next moves.

CHAPTER **28**

I Wasn't Even Tired

(Lesson Two from Chapter 26)

I firmly believe that any man's finest hour, the greatest fulfillment of all that he holds dear, is that moment when he has worked his heart out in a good cause and lies exhausted on the field of battle—victorious.

—*Vince Lombardi*

I do not think that anyone can say it better than Vince Lombardi. When we work at something we believe in, our passion drives us to exhaustion. I hope that everyone reading these words has had that experience. When it is compared to the mind set of those that stand by idle, the contrast is stark. Like most of you, I have had times when my mind and body were idle, and I do not like what I felt and saw in myself. If you do not believe in the fight, it is just work, and your efforts will be far less than those you produce when you are passionate about the results.

As the co-owner of a water park, I was constantly aware of our efforts to keep the park clean for our guests. One day while walking around the park I noticed two young staff members slowly walking along the sidewalk chatting, and every now and then stopping to sweep up some litter. Clearly they were more interested in talking with each other than keeping the park clean. At the same time, I would not hesitate to run around the food area cleaning up ketchup spills and bussing tables without thinking of anything but making it look nice and clean for our guests. I was invested in the mission of the park, and I had not done a good enough job in helping some of my staff understand and catch that vision.

You can HighFive Your Life by making sure that you exhaust yourself in the passion of life. If you are not exhausted, it may be wise to take a look at what you are doing to make sure that it is a work in which you believe. Make the adjustment. Find "your finest hour" by working your heart out in a cause that is dear to you.

HighFive Your Life Principle

Exhaust yourself in the passion of your life. If you are not doing this you need to find your passion.

CHAPTER 29

Will We See a Replay?

(Lesson Three from Chapter 26)

Criticism may not be agreeable, but it is necessary. It fulfills the same function as pain in the human body. It calls attention to an unhealthy state of things.
—*Winston Churchill*

For many sporting events in your life, you are going to get to see a replay. With the ease of digital filming now, every parent has a closet full of their kid's soccer and football exploits. My football coach at Princeton used to keep track of each play in each game so that when we reviewed it on the films, we could see what we had done correctly and incorrectly. A day or two after the game we would gather as a team to review the films. He would give each of us a card that had the play number and his comments, and then follow with words of encouragement to do better the next week. Although sometimes the comments seemed harsh, I will be forever grateful for that attention that he gave us. It helped us improve our individual performance as the season progressed. I kept some of those cards in a scrapbook and have included them in this chapter.

I have also known those that do not like to see a replay, that do not see the critique as helpful and are not interested in using the past to improve the future. It is one thing to consider and debate when discussing sports. It is another to consider when discussing life. I for one believe that we often have an opportunity to improve when we have a good attitude about our performance critique. Sometimes it may be hard, but you can HighFive Your Life by considering a performance critique not as an evaluation of your worth, but as a great look at things from someone with a different perspective. For those that believe in a hereafter, you may have an opportunity one day to see the "great replay in the sky." Are you looking forward to that viewing?

Larson — Harvard '77
77 +   2 —

Play # 5   Get better piece of your man when blocking.

Play # 42   Get better position on man.

Play # 47   Hang onto ball we were lucky on your fumble.

Play # 80   On 36 Belly <u>Downs</u> look to bounce it out side of wings block.

Play # 83   Poor block.

Gary,
Don't be down on your performance. You did a lot of good things out there. We proved to ourselves that we can win the big games. Let's continue to work hard and improve on our performance's. We have to get ready for this Penn group. They'll be sky-hi for us. If we're not ready they'll kick the stuff right out of us. Make sure we are ready to play our game.

Larson — Brown '77
44 +   6 —

Play # 10   When fill blocking, get into man.

Play # 21   Keep feet when blocking.

Play # 30   You look confused?

Play # 34   You look like you are not ready for block.

Play # 46   More "pop" on your block.

Play # 47   Good job of eying stunting LB'er get him if you decide too.

Play # 58   Poor block. You leave your feet.

Play # 68   You miss everyone. Run up to their toes and then explode into them. You seem to be diving at people here.

Gary,
This is the best job by any fullback that I've ever seen here. Sure you made a few errors but it's nothing that can't be corrected. It was a great effort. Your ball carrying is getting better each week. Keep up the good work. I'm not allowing myself as a coach to get down and I know you won't. Let's continue to work hard and prepare for this week's game vs Columbia.

As my wife and I were raising our children we found that we were generally in agreement with how we should handle disciplining them. However, we also felt overwhelmed with the constant daily occurrences where discipline of some sort was needed. Sometimes we felt like we did not do as well as we should have. We watched other parents and how they handled their children and discussed what we liked and didn't like about what they did. Finally we spoke from time to time with our own parents and got ideas from them. The bottom line is that we accepted outside influences to help us improve how we handled our children.

Larson – Columbia '77

4A + 7 –

Play# 9 Bad position for block

Play# 12 Fill on trap

Play# 17 No minus but keep feet on block.

Play# 18 You miss man.

Play# 19 Don't know what the problem is but we fumble ball. Let's get it corrected.

Play #27 Poor block. You can do better.

Play #28 Poor block again. Must improve

Play #29 Good block!! Do it like that every time.

Play# 30 Gave you two tt's Great job!

Larson – Penn '77

17 + 1 –

Play# 3 Great block. Bone Crusher!

Play #17 Look confused and ended up blocking no one. Get into 1st off colored jersey.

Gary,
    You were having a fine day. I'm sorry you had to come up with that pull. Make sure you take care of that leg. We hope you are capable of

Play # 40 Get lower when fill blocking.

Play # 55 No minus but you might be able to get up 4 over.

Gary,
    Our first win made us all feel good. We have the biggest challenge this week. We are going to beat them but we have to continue to work hard and prepare well. They are rated #1 Team in East. What a trophy a win over them will be. Our offense has to control ball. We will and we'll beat them. Good game last week but let's make this one even better.

playing some more this year. We were all "down" after the Penn game but that's natural. To stay "down" is not natural unless we are quitters and I know we are not so pick your head up and we'll get our butts in gear and go after there Yale people. We can do it!!

Nobody likes to be told what to do. Nobody likes to be forced into receiving advice. Be so confident in what you are doing that you beat the advice givers to the punch. Ask for advice! Filter it. Take the best wisdom that applies to your situation and keep moving.

HighFive Your Life Principle

A performance critique is not an evaluation of the worth of your soul, but may be very helpful in improving your performance. Don't just leave it to chance; seek out this critique.

CHAPTER 30

I Want a Rematch

(Lesson Four from Chapter 26)

He has spent all his life in letting down empty buckets into empty wells; and he is frittering away his age in trying to draw them up again.
—*Sydney Smith*

How many of us have wished that we could do something over again? Sometimes we get that opportunity, but many times we don't. For some reason we tend to think that there will be more time to get it right in the end. If we assume that we will have another opportunity we may not give it our all the first time.

We need to fight as if there were no such thing as a rematch. When we get to the Pearly Gates it is a little late to want to put on the gloves. This is the time to fight your fight. This is the time to do what you want to do with your life. This is your turn to make your time on this earth mean something.

You can HighFive Your Life by living it to its fullest each day with the thought in mind that this is your fight, your time in the ring. Leave it all in the ring. There are no rematches.

HighFive Your Life Principle

Fight your fight today.

CHAPTER 31

At the End of Your Round, Go to Your Corner

(Lesson Five from Chapter 26)

Courage is what it takes to stand up and speak; courage is also what it takes to sit down and listen.
—*Winston Churchill*

You can be the heavyweight champion of the world and know everything there is to know about boxing and be in the best shape of your life, but you still go to your corner between rounds. Each round is three minutes and then you are given one minute in your corner. Your corner is a place where many important things happen in a very short period of time, and a place where a boxer finds relief from the fight.

In your corner, you always have your trainer. The trainer sees the fight through a different pair of eyes. He not only sees your opponent but he sees you and how you are responding to your opponent. He knows from countless hours of training what your strengths and weaknesses are, and in the fight he knows which ones are manifesting themselves. Your trainer tells you whether you are winning or losing. He tells you how to improve or change your strategy. A smart fighter listens to his trainer because in the heat of the battle, a different perspective helps. He provides balance. He provides encouragement.

During a three minute round you expend all your energy and take a pounding. In your corner, your cuts and bruises are given attention. You are rehydrated. You rest. When the bell rings you come out ready to go to war again. Your corner is sometimes your best weapon.

You can HighFive Your Life by recognizing first that you need to have a corner, and then making sure that you visit there often between the rounds of life. From whom do you to seek direction? Are you so hardheaded that you think you have it all figured out and don't need input from anybody?

I have found that the perspective that others offer oftentimes has helped me even when it was not solicited or welcomed by me. It may come from a parent or spouse, a coach or employer, a priest or a friend. It may come from a good book or inspiration during meditation. Each of us needs a corner. Each of us needs a place to gain others' perspectives on our lives. Each of us needs to have our cuts and bruises attended to, and each of us needs to rest. Those that are fooled into thinking that they are beyond this principle of life miss a great opportunity to find peace and direction. HighFive Your Life by finding your corner and going there often.

HighFive Your Life Principle

Find your place where you can go to get good counsel, rest, and healing, and don't let anything or anybody keep you from getting there.

CHAPTER 32

Sometimes You Need to Be the Trainer in the Corner

(Lesson Six from Chapter 26)

The more tranquil a man becomes, the greater is his success, his influence, his power for good. Calmness of mind is one of the beautiful jewels of wisdom.
—*James Allen*

Each of us can count the people that have been there for us when we needed them. They are the people that we never forget. When we have issues that we want to discuss, or that we can't resolve, we go to them and feel better. They are our trainers when we need them, and we are forever grateful to them.

Sometimes people come to each of us and ask for advice and counsel. We each do our best to try and offer whatever nuggets of wisdom that we have mined along the way. We feel good to be in a position to help, and the people asking for our help are grateful. What about when we think we need to offer advice but are sure that the recipient isn't going to appreciate it? Are we strong enough to give guidance when it is not welcomed?

I think that you can HighFive Your Life by having the wisdom and courage to speak your mind when needed, even when that counsel is not requested. Sometimes we need to be the trainer and do the training. It takes some balance to not be overbearing, but outspoken counsel, when it is easier to just say nothing, is the kind of openness that is missing in many families and friendships. It is missing because it sometimes seems just too hard to do. It can damage a relationship in the short term.

It can cause emotional stress for everybody involved. Honest communication requires effort and thought on the part of the advice giver.

One day when I was in my early twenties and home from college, I spent some time with my girlfriend who lived about an hour from my family's home. It was the Christmas season and it was just an exciting time to be home. I had picked her up and we were driving down a dark, two-lane country road with orange groves all around us. I noticed that the car in front of us was weaving back and forth across the middle of the road. It looked clearly like something was wrong. All I could think about was that this guy was going to run head on into some car coming from the other direction filled with a family excited about Christmas and kill them all.

There was not much I could do so I started flashing my lights at him. I'm not sure what I was expecting, but I wondered if he might be falling asleep and thought it might get his attention. I was surprised when he started slowing down and then pulled off the road. I decided I had better pull off, too. I walked back to the car to see if he was okay and he gave me one of those classic "Occifer Occifer" lines thinking that I was a police officer. He was so drunk he could hardly speak. I assured him that I was not a cop and asked if I could give him a ride somewhere. He was an older man and I can't imagine what I was thinking to invite a strange old drunk man into my car with my girlfriend in the back orange groves on some country road! I guess I was not thinking.

He agreed that I could give him a ride back to the bar in town. I asked if there was someone we could call to pick up the car and he said that it was not his. We all got in my car and drove to the bar. There was no such thing as a cell phone at this time so after letting him out, we drove to the convenience store and called the police on the pay phone. I told them that we thought we had found a stolen car. They came out and we all went out to the car. They ran a check and sure enough it had just been reported stolen. The officer started asking us all kinds of details about the man and I could not remember much, but my girlfriend remembered everything (That should have been a clue about what to expect in married life). They asked if we would go back to the bar and identify him and we agreed. We parked across the street from the bar and they soon brought him out and we gave them the sign. Undercover police had found him inside trying to sell prescription medication.

All in all it was a pretty exciting evening. I was worried enough about the consequences of doing nothing that I did all I could do on that dark country road. I blinked my lights. Because I did that, other opportunities to solve the problem emerged. Because I blinked my lights, I feel like we saved a family from a deadly head-on collision, found a stolen car, and got somebody off the street who was selling drugs.

There are many people, especially among our families and friends, that need to have lights blinked at them every now and then. Our children are especially in need. It does not have to be a blinding search light in their eyes, but it should be something that gets their attention.

It could be a warning about their health, like when my friend whom I respected very much told me that I weighed too much and was risking death and that I meant too much to him to let me die. I ran for over 900 straight days after that conversation.

It could be forcing your teenager to be home at a specific time or not letting kids see certain movies that their friends are seeing. It could be counsel to be less sloppy or to manage your money better. It could be counsel to forgive. It could be instructions on how to be a better spouse, and sometimes those instructions may come from your spouse.

Generally, when someone is flashing their lights at us we do not want to see them. However, when it is done with respect and true concern, it eventually sinks in. There is a great difference between nagging and pestering, and giving good counsel. There is also a time, especially with children, where there is no negotiation required. Ours is the opportunity to learn best how to give counsel when it is needed but not requested. High-Five Your Life and that of your family and friends by being brave enough to give loving counsel when it is needed.

HighFive Your Life Principle

Be brave enough to give loving counsel when needed.

CHAPTER 33

You Can't Lose All by Yourself

(Lesson Seven from Chapter 26)

There's nothing terribly wrong with feeling lost, so long as that feeling precedes some plan on your part to actually do something about it. Too often a person grows complacent with their disillusionment, perpetually wearing their "discomfort" like a favorite shirt.

—*Jhonen Vasquez*

As we travel through life, we may get the feeling that when we lose it only affects us. If we believe that, we make a big mistake. When people become isolationists and feel like they want to be left alone because for some reason they have given up the fight, it doesn't just affect them. It ripples through the whole family or set of friends.

We all lose at something sometime in our lives. Most of us lose at many things. Failure may seem lonely. Nobody wants to be there. However, you are loved by those around you and your life experiences matter to them. You can HighFive Your Life by knowing that your fight in life is actually much more than just about you. People are counting on you. Your personal losses have an impact on others. Keep fighting even if it feels like you are alone in your struggles. Know that you are part of a plan that is much bigger than you. Do your part.

If you find yourself in a pattern of life that seems to be chalking up more losses than wins, stop and gather yourself. Evaluate your situation. Break it down into smaller understandable parts. Seek wisdom. Work. Mess up. Try again. Work. Pray. Write in your journal. Mess up. Work. Seek wisdom. Pray. Help somebody else. Work. Forgive. Get up earlier. Work. Seek wisdom. Laugh. Laugh at yourself. Pray. Be kind to somebody. Look at the stars. Write in your journal. Know your journey is part of the plan. Move forward.

Little by little, step by step, take control of your life and play the game that you were meant to play. Know that the world is better because you are in it. Know that you are loved. Desire to do your part. Do your part.

HighFive Your Life Principle

Don't be fooled into thinking that you are alone in your struggles. Your life matters to many, even if it does not seem that way. People need you. Do your part.

CHAPTER 34

Feeling Important?

Indispensable Man

Sometime when you're feeling important,
Sometime when your ego's in bloom,
Sometime when you take it for granted,
You're the best qualified in the room;
Sometime when you feel that your going
Would leave an unfillable hole,
Just follow these simple instructions
And see how they humble your soul.
Take a bucket and fill it with water
Put your hand in it up to the wrist,
Pull it out and the hole that's remaining
Is the measure of how you'll be missed.
You can splash all you want when you enter,
You may stir up the water galore;
But stop, and you'll find that in no time
It looks quite the same as before.
The moral in this quaint example
Is to do just the best that you can;
Be proud of yourself, but remember
There's no indispensable man.

—*Saxon White Kessinger*

One of the great principles to balance in your life is that of pride. We should all be proud of our work, have solid self-esteem, and generally have a positive attitude about our very existence. However, when we begin to determine that we are somehow just a little more special than everyone else, we begin to creep onto the slippery slope of being too prideful and overconfident.

Nobody really likes to be around somebody who turns their personal confidence into a statement of superiority. Nobody has been made perfect and, though a person may have some very special gifts such as good looks, a great voice, or some incredible talent, they also have been given special weaknesses. Nobody is immune, even if the world in a moment of adoration seems to forget, forgive and ignore those weaknesses. It is not uncommon for those that have to deal with their special gifts to have trouble keeping some sort of balance in their lives in order to find true happiness and peace of mind.

I for one, have not had that problem. Even though I have been blessed with a fairly mediocre and common look and no singing voice or great talent to speak of, I have had to learn the hard way not to take myself too seriously. Despite the ordinariness that each one of us generally has, we also generally have something that we are pretty good at, if we apply ourselves. It is in those times, when I have succeeded sufficiently in some form or fashion to begin to bask in my success, that I have been struck down to the ground and left to wander listlessly in my exposed pedestrian way, until I have been able to regain sufficient composure to get up and get going again.

The result of the lessons that I have learned is that when I notice that I am starting to think that I am pretty special in a certain way, all kinds of bells and whistles go off inside my head and I almost want to duck. I find myself in a prayer that goes something like this: Heavenly Father, I realize what I was thinking wasn't quite right and please don't feel the need to remind me. I get it! With some hesitancy I share a few of the examples in my life that have lead me to react this way.

Sometime in my early forties, my wife and I went to the annual Chamber of Commerce party in a fancy hotel ballroom in Central Florida. This was a big deal. Everybody was dressed up, and they had dinner and dancing and gave away a car at the end of the night. At this stage in my business career, I was feeling pretty confident. Our water park, Water Mania, had been open for at least a decade and was becoming part of the attractions industry landscape. I had married way over my head and had four beautiful children. I did not get out much, but for some reason this night, I was feeling pretty good about myself.

That night I learned one lesson right off the bat, and that was to never again enter an auction for a dozen roses. It came down to a bidding war between me and another man with both of our wives watching. How stupid is that? I had to just keep bidding because I did not want to be the one that didn't give it all for my spouse. I finally won but it cost me several hundred dollars. Thank goodness that the other man was comfortable enough with himself and his wife not to be fooled into continuing in the "bidding for show" in which I was engaged.

After a lot fun, dancing, and mingling, the evening was finally drawing to a close. As my wife and I left the ballroom, I stopped by the men's room for some relief before the drive home. I am not going to go into details but suffice it to say that I had a once in a lifetime accident and wet my pants all over the front. That's right, the guy that was standing so tall and proud just a few minutes before was now trying to get out to the car without everyone seeing the mishap that had just happened. My bubble burst, and I was reminded of just who I was and who I wasn't.

At another point in my life, I had the opportunity to caddie for my college roommate turned PGA professional in a local golf tournament. I had caddied several times before on the PGA tour with him and knew pretty much what I was doing. Now at this second tier tournament, it was obvious that the same caliber of caddies was not being utilized as those at a full PGA event. On the final day of play, I remember arriving at the golf course with my buddy and reflecting on really how much better I was than the other caddies. I remember actually wondering if any of the other pro golfers were wondering where my friend had picked up such a great caddie as I thought myself to be.

Today such thinking would set off warning bells, but not so then. I still had not learned. Somewhere on the back nine, my friend hit a long drive into a fairway bunker. It skipped several times over 20 feet or so and made several marks in the sand. As we approached the bunker, being the very efficient caddie that I was, I picked up the rake and thought I would rake the first of the marks away so that I would not have to do it after his shot. Just inches before the rake hit the sand he yelled out to stop me. I retracted the rake and he told me that it would have been a penalty had I touched the sand. He made his shot and I humbly raked the sand like a dutiful hired caddy.

As we were driving home at the end of the tournament, I asked him what would have happened if I had actually raked the sand. He said that he would have called for a referee to come out and make a decision which would have stopped play for several minutes. It could have cost him a couple of strokes, which would have been horrible. What also stung was the thought that up on the green among the group of people waiting for the golfers to hit, I could easily imagine a conversation going something like this: "What is happening? Why doesn't he hit his ball?" To which another person would have responded: "You didn't hear; his dimwit caddie raked the sand before he hit and it cost him a couple of strokes. I wonder where he found that loser of a caddie." Needless to say I was quite relieved that I had not raked the sand, but I had still learned this lesson again the hard way.

Let me share one last example of why I tend to be wary when my "ego is in bloom" as the poem says.

As I discussed in an earlier chapter, a buddy invited me to go to a ten-day motivational seminar with him in Hawaii. We stayed at a nice resort and in the evening attended the opening ceremonies. There was a lot of drum beating and loud music and everyone's adrenaline was high. After some introductory remarks, we were told that we would be put into assigned groups and were released to find our group marker. We were then told that we would be divided up into a companionship and that this would be the partner with whom we would experience the balance of the time at the seminar. We were told to be bold and not choose a partner that we came with, but to get the full value of the seminar by choosing a different and new companion. Well, I was not interested in that at all and was not worried because my friend and I were buddies, and we were going to have a great time working on getting better on a lot of individual things together.

The leader then told us that the way we would choose our partner would be to look around with our eyes and try and find someone who was staring back at you. If they stared at you that meant that they wanted to be your partner. If they turned their head, that meant that you were rejected and you needed to find someone else. Again, I was not worried because my friend and I were partners. The leader said "go" and it became mayhem as everyone scrambled to find a partner. We stood up and stared at each other and I said, "Well, I guess we're partners."

No sooner had those words left my lips than a cute lady stepped between us and said, "No, he is my partner." We were both shocked. It turns out that she had seen him on the airplane coming over to Hawaii and perhaps I haven't mentioned it yet, but he is drop-dead good looking.

There was some hesitation on his part as we stood there staring at each other not knowing what to do. Within seconds though, the answer became obvious. I was on my own! I had come to Hawaii a very confident man that just wanted to work on my health a little and hang out with my buddy. I had a nice business and family and wasn't really looking for a life-changing experience. I was very confident. Now all of a sudden as I turned to face the mayhem behind me I saw that nobody was staring at me. Nobody wanted me. I felt like the first grade kid who was picked last for the kickball team. Finally, I raced through the group and intercepted some guy that was streaking across the room, stared him down, and said we are going to be partners. He agreed. That was the highlight of this new partnership and it went downhill from there. He was there for a life-changing event and I just wanted to be with my friend and work on my health. When it came to divulging all my inner fears and weaknesses to this stranger as the curriculum encouraged you to do, I was not a very willing participant. After several days, he wanted out and I was all too happy to oblige.

My point with these stories is that you HighFive Your Life when you don't get too caught up in yourself. We should all have pride in what we do but, as with all principles, there needs to be a balance. The moment we begin to think we are just something a little more special in God's view than the next person, we are setting ourselves up for a humbling reminder of our humanity. I, for one, have learned my lesson and I didn't even share all of these types of experiences with you. I love my life but recognize that God loves all of our lives. I am a very competitive person. If you challenge me we will get it on right there. However, I also try to remember both the wise old owl and the reminders from above. We need to do the best we can always and feel good with a job well done, but we should always remember the lesson in the poem and know that there is no indispensable man.

HighFive Your Life Principle

Do the best that you can in all things, but be careful when your pride starts to get in the way. Generally, life reminds us that humble pie is an entree served all too often when the appetizer has been pride.

CHAPTER 35

Don't Let the Stars Line Up Against You

You've got to be very careful if you don't know where you're going, because you might not get there.

—*Yogi Berra*

It was on another RV trip that I learned another very important lesson in life. Sometimes things that go really bad can be prevented by just a few small adjustments beforehand. We were in the West when we stopped at a campground and took down the bikes for our young kids to ride. My youngest child and only daughter, Allie, complained that her hand brakes were not releasing correctly, making it hard to ride. Additionally, the seat was too low and needed to be raised. I worked on the hand brakes for awhile to no avail, so I decided to just undo them. After all, the bike still had pedal brakes, which seemed sufficient to me. I also raised the seat for her.

All seemed well that evening. The next morning we had a pancake breakfast and decided to go on a walk; that is, my wife and I would walk while the kids rode their bikes. We started with the kids going ahead of us, and Joey and I bringing up the rear engaged in some conversation which I do not remember, but I am sure it had something to do with how much she loved and adored me.

What I do remember is that suddenly our conversation was interrupted by a bloodcurdling scream. We looked up and the kids had decided to go down a very steep hill that led to a lower parking area at the campground. At the bottom of the hill was a hairpin right turn that then opened up into another RV parking lot. Beyond the turn, straight downhill, was a cliff that dropped about 20 feet into a wooded area.

The instant I heard my little girl's scream I started off in a sprint, but there was no catching her. Without her hand brakes she had to depend on the foot brakes to slow her down. The problem was that she was going so fast that her feet could not stay on the pedals to brake them. Additionally, because I had raised her seat, she could not reach down with her feet to try and stop herself. It was a horribly helpless feeling as I raced after her with no hope of catching her.

As she reached the bottom and disappeared out of our sight, there was a deafening silence for one or two seconds and then a loud wailing. We got to the bottom and were so relieved to find that she had crashed into a debris pile someone had left just before the edge of the cliff. She was cut and scared but otherwise okay. Joey and I were somewhat in shock at what had just happened, but humbled and grateful.

Not only had she not been hit by an RV that could have been pulling out of the parking lot at anytime, she had been saved by the debris pile from going over the cliff. That day the stars had come pretty close to lining up for a disaster, and we all felt that we were fortunate with the outcome. The things that I had done—raising her seat, dismantling the hand brake, and engaging in conversation with my wife—taken by themselves seemed to be somewhat unimportant. However, taken together they were just one brush pile, or one RV leaving the lot, away from disaster.

You cannot HighFive Your Life by living in fear of what is waiting down the road all the time. But, we can be careful to be aware of small details that when put together with other small details, lend themselves to disaster. A great example is drinking and driving.

Think of two or three things that need to happen for this to lead to a disaster. It is easy. First of all, one needs to be drinking. Second, one needs to not have a designated driver in place. Third, the one drinking just needs to think that he can get home without assistance. With those three factors, a downhill collision course has been set up.

You can HighFive Your Life by examining your own life and the lives of those you love to see where you can set up simple guideposts that will reduce the possibility of the stars lining up. Things like having the kids come home at a certain time, not being left alone in an unfamiliar place, having a phone with you in your car, or knowing what to do when you have a flat tire in the middle of nowhere.

Finally, in the example of my daughter, after all else failed on my part, the debris pile left by someone else possibly saved my girl's life. We never know how the things we do in life may impact others. You may be the safety net for someone around you that is tumbling down the hill out of control. The debris pile that saved my daughter did not have to perform some great insightful miracle or express incredible words of wisdom and instruction. It just had to be there. You can HighFive Your Life and the lives of those we love sometimes by just being there.

HighFive Your Life Principle

Be careful to watch out for the small details of life that, when connected together into a string of events, can cause a much bigger problem and maybe even a disaster.

Chapter 36

Daddy Hold Me

If there must be trouble, let it be in my day, that my child may have peace.
—*Thomas Paine*

Those words will forever haunt me. Not because they are not sweet words—on the contrary, there are no sweeter words—but because of how I responded when I heard them. The event was so seared into my soul that I actually took the time to write the experience down some twenty-plus years ago. The following is that story:

> I missed it. I can't believe I missed it. As I lay next to my almost three year old boy on the air mattress I wanted to wake him and talk to him. That sweet moment that I had been looking forward to, that of snuggling together and talking and laughing, was what had made me most excited about going to my first father/son campout.
>
> His innocence and curiosity is often expressed so clearly and sweetly as we lie together when I put him to bed. I knew with all of the excitement of the day that tonight lying on that air mattress in the tent would have been especially sweet and fun. But here I was awake, just looking at my boy sleeping. How I missed that opportunity. . . . and then it just hit me . . . I really did miss that opportunity.
>
> Our first father/son outing, which my church does annually, had begun the previous week when we went shopping and bought the necessary gear. Of course, we had to practice setting up the tent in our living room, which I won't do again. For some reason, 20 foot flexible rods bent under tension don't complement an arrangement of a large TV, piano, and couch. And of course, two of my three sons under the age of

three couldn't understand why this wasn't their fort for life and had to be taken down.

The day arrived with great anticipation on my part. I came home from work early and while Robbie (my oldest) napped, I packed up all of the necessary gear that would insure our survival for the next 15 hours—tent, pillows, air mattress, Swiss knife, potato chips, flashlights (an assortment of three sizes plus a lantern), guitar, marshmallows, hammer, chair, warm clothes, bug repellant, and of course directions to the place we were going.

When I woke him, the excitement that generally only comes on Christmas morning was there. The van was loaded so off we went . . . two men to face the wilds together.

I hadn't gone a half mile and I realized how excited I must have been because I began to remember things that I had forgotten . . . Robbie's chair, an alarm clock and oh no!. . . . not my cooler with drinks. I called home and my wife agreed to take care of my error.

It was about 5:15 P.M. when we arrived and being among the first, we analyzed the real estate and strategically located ourselves by both the bathroom and the food. Robbie and I immediately began putting up our tent and as he helped me hammer in the stakes, the desires of my heart began to be fulfilled. Here I was a father with my little boy camping . . . It seemed so simple and yet so fulfilling and wonderful. I looked forward to those moments we would share together as we lay down to sleep later that night . . . father and son overcoming the wilderness and finding security in each other.

There was much to happen before that opportunity came. As others began to arrive, I realized that Robbie was much more interested in playing and running with his little friends and that my job for the evening was to be one of coach, security guard and chaser-after. I soon learned that although the Star Wars light-up-in-the-dark sword I had brought for him was neat, it didn't come close to being equal with the bats, balls, and gloves the other boys had. I learned my first lesson in father/son outings. . . . .bring what your boy really wants to play with not what you think he will want to play with.

Finally, after much eating, running, and sitting around a bonfire etc., the time drew near when we would lay down together on that air mattress and talk about things that fathers and their almost-3-year-old sons discuss.

Just before we entered the tent at about 11:00 P.M., I decided to load some of the things back in the van since we had to leave early the next morning. To my dismay the van was locked and the keys were inside. I called my wife but couldn't reach her. My friend Ed offered me a ride to my house so we could get the spare which I finally accepted. I asked another friend Keith who was there with his son Ryan to keep Robbie awake until I returned.

After a frantic search at my home, I realized that the spare was also inside the van. I grabbed some sheets with the full intent to smash one of the windows. Ed convinced me to at least try a hanger first.

When we returned, Robbie was still awake running around in the damp air in his underwear with no shirt or shoes . . . not a good idea but this was training for manhood right?

I concentrated on the van . . . one hour went by . . . I sat Robbie on the ground wrapped in the sheets I had brought. We continued working and working to get the hanger to catch the lock. I noticed Robbie sitting very still and sleepy. How pitiful he looked . . . but we weren't having much luck and I got madder and madder.

Finally Robbie said, "Daddy hold me." My friend Jim picked him up and I kept on working on the van. Soon Jim laid him in the tent and a little while later we got into the van. I could finally go lay down with my son . . . but he was fast asleep. I lay there looking at Robbie, yearning for him to be awake and to talk with me, and then it hit me, I had missed it. I had been looking forward to cuddling and loving Robbie on my terms . . . that is, when we lay down to sleep and yet he had offered it on his terms when he said, "Daddy hold me." I just missed it. As I lay there in that dark tent, I wished so much that I had dropped everything and held that little boy when he had asked me to.

We packed up at about 5:00 A.M. cold and damp. Robbie was still sleeping when I laid him down in his own bed. Our trip concluded, I am already thinking about next year. I will bring the ball and bat, leave the glowing sword and hope I'll have the chance to hear one more time "Daddy hold me."

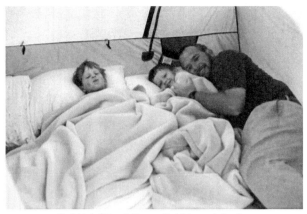

Robbie's friend Ryan, Robbie and Author

You and I have special moments that are happening around us all of the time. The stress of schedules and work and sometimes the lapse in judgment regarding what is important place us in a position to overlook or not recognize those moments when they are occurring.

You can HighFive Your Life by looking for those special moments, those HighFive Moments, and making yourself become sensitive to them. As they occur, you may or may not need to change your actions or behavior. As you recognize them, however, you will find a little increase in joy just for being in the zone with what is most important.

HighFive Your Life Principle

Don't be a dummy like I was. Look for the special moments and hold on to them.

Chapter 37

Enjoy Problem Solving

It's not that I'm so smart, it's just that I stay with problems longer.
—Albert Einstein

My father enjoyed taking his two sons hunting when the opportunity presented itself, but in reality it didn't happen very often when I was growing up. As I went off to college, my father joined a hunting lease that allowed him to hunt on about 21,000 acres. It was great bringing my northern college friends home over break to take them hog hunting. We have some great memories from that hunting camp.

One day my father and brother and I were riding in the hunting Jeep on a dirt road far from camp. All of a sudden the right rear axle broke and the Jeep came to a stop. It is not an unusual experience to get a Jeep stuck in a Florida swamp followed by long walks back to camp. But we were not stuck, we were just broken down.

I have always been proud of myself that I helped solve that problem. We took the cable from the winch on the front of the Jeep and wrapped it backwards around the roll bar on the left side of the Jeep and then across the back of the Jeep, connecting it to the right rear axle. A quick crank by the winch and the axle was off the ground. We then put the Jeep in four wheel drive and, if I stood on the front bumper to give it some weight, we found that we could slowly make our way back to camp. Other than my dad and I getting in a verbal joust when I thought he was going to kill me as we went through a creek bed and he almost ran over me, we made it back fine.

On the other hand, recently my wife and I went to dinner with another couple and when we returned to the car, my electronic key did not work. We were stuck. Using my best training as an engineer from Princeton, I beat the key, banged the key, shook the key—basically did anything I could think of to try and get it to miraculously work just one last time. Finally my wife asked if the valet key would work that was in the console of the car. I was such a dummy. It worked just great and we were soon on our way. I hate to say it, but trying to get the shower to work at a hotel in Europe was just as challenging. Once again, my wife figured it out before me.

When I am faced with a problem that is not easily solved, it very quickly turns into a challenge to solve it. I am not looking for problems and I prefer not to have them. However, we all know they will come and when they do, you can HighFive Your Life by taking a deep breath and engaging yourself with the right attitude to solve them.

Problem solving is like a sport. Approach a problem that way. It's you against the problem with just seconds on the clock . . . What are you going to do? . . . Are you going to make the shot? . . . How are you going to solve it? . . . The crowd is cheering . . . What is your move?

I have now learned that the best thing to do is just pass the problem off to my wife and let her win the game. She has the best shot out of all of us!

HighFive Your Life Principle

When presented with a problem, accept it as a challenge to solve instead of just another obstacle to prevent you from getting where you want to be. Find joy in the fact that you solved it, and then move on to the next problem.

CHAPTER 38

You Owe It ... Not Me

Liberty means responsibility. That is why most men dread it.
—*George Bernard Shaw*

I visited a hardware store and while shopping, noticed a man that I thought was trying to put a large roll of wire mesh back up on a high shelf. I started helping him but soon realized he was not lifting but instead pulling it down to his cart below. When it came down it caught my finger between the mesh and cart and opened a huge cut on my knuckle. We both stared at the wound and he offered to drive me to the emergency room.

Though it was gaping open, for some reason it wasn't bleeding. I told him I could drive myself and turned to leave. I made it all the way back to the checkout stand where all the contractors were standing and I began to get woozy. The next thing I knew, I was flat on my back and hearing someone say that an ambulance was on the way. I came to my senses and told them to call off the ambulance, that I was okay. I recovered sufficiently to drive to the ER and get stitches and go home. Other than embarrassing the family name by fainting in front of the local construction people, I was fine.

Soon thereafter, I received a bill from the hospital for several hundred dollars for my ER visit. At the time I was in my mid-twenties and managing one of my parent's two hotels. Our insurance policy at the hotel had a provision where we were directed to pay for any injury under $1000 without questions. If there was a fall or a twisted ankle or any other small injury on the hotel property, we were to send them to a clinic and pay for it regardless of whose fault it was.

This insurance arrangement came to mind when I received the bill and I assumed that the hardware store must have something similar. I argued to myself that I was actually trying to help their customer when I was injured and therefore they should be willing to pay for my ER visit. I am not sure how my mother found out about my plans to submit the bill to the hardware store but I will never forget her reaction when she did find out.

She came to my bachelor pad and began to chew me out. Though I do not recall her exact words, she basically said that it was not the hardware store's fault that I had my finger in the wrong place and that it was my responsibility not theirs. This was not an exchange of ideas or pleasantries between Mom and me. I put up a feeble argument, but she was on point, passionate and, by the way, correct. I paid the bill.

In this day and age when the tendency is to look for someone else to blame, you can HighFive Your life by taking full responsibility for your actions. It is a breath of fresh air when you see somebody do it. It is an uplifting feeling when you hear somebody say it. Whether it is a dropped pass and the receiver says "my bad," or a co-worker who recognizes their error and works to correct it, the sensation that is given to those around by someone who is taking responsibility for their actions is a massive lift.

There are also many opportunities to take responsibility for your actions when few if any will know the difference. These are subtle but character building, and should not be overlooked. If you drop a paper towel on the floor after washing your hands in a public bathroom do you pick it up or just leave it? Do you return what you borrowed in a condition that is at least as good if not better than when you borrowed it? Do you throw away your empty popcorn bags and drink cups after watching a good movie in a theatre? Do you pick up your dirty socks and clothes? Do you leave your dirty dishes for someone else? If you stay at somebody's house over night, before you leave do you take the used linens to their washer to be cleaned? They may tell you that it is not necessary, but most likely will appreciate the gesture.

I have had moments of irresponsibility in my life, but have had a desire to do better as I have grown older. As a society, we will be much better off when we as individuals take responsibility for our actions.

HighFive Your Life Principle

Take full responsibility for your actions whether seen or unseen. Make it a personal choice.

CHAPTER 39

The Magic Box Called Forgiveness

Forgiveness is the fragrance that the violet sheds on the heel that has crushed it.
—*Mark Twain*

How often has each of us been offended or hurt by something that someone else has said or done? It seems to happen daily or weekly and becomes the subject of many heartfelt conversations among close friends and family members. Sometimes the situations slowly seem to ebb away. Sometimes a direct conversation between the two people involved results in an apology or at least an understanding.

But every now and then, a situation becomes so extreme that there seems to be no possible way to get over it. You reach a point where there is such an impasse that there seems to be no hope for any resolution. It bites at you throughout the day and week and month. A wonderful Sunday afternoon with the family can turn sour if you happen to let the thought of the issue cross your mind. The injustice of the offense is just too much to bear.

Much has been written regarding forgiveness. It is, of course, easy to talk to someone about it or encourage someone to do it when you are not the person that is feeling the pain. When the pain is yours, however, forgiving another may just seem too much to consider. At times it seems hard to hold onto the belief that each soul has value, and that we should love our enemies.

My experiences with this have been painful. How can I love them when I have been hurt so much? How can I love them when I feel to the core that an injustice has been done? How can I love them when I think I am right and they are wrong?

When I had this experience in the past, I knew that I should be more tolerant and should forgive as God has told us to do. It was just so hard. From a very practical perspective, I just had a hard time getting it done. I do not know where I was when the answer came to me after months and years of dealing with this burden. Perhaps it is a cheater's way of forgiving, but it worked for me. I simply created this little box in my head where I decided to place things that I would never understand nor ever have to understand. As I figuratively placed this hard-to-understand issue in this box, I could not believe the weight that was lifted off of me. To my surprise, I found that suddenly I was able to feel love again.

As I have grown older, I realize that Jesus lives in that box. However, if your belief system does not take you there, that's okay; just place it in the box anyway. It works.

Over time, you may realize that some of the blame in those heartfelt and tough situations was your fault. I did. As we all know, there are two sides to every story. Conflicts between neighbors, spouses, friends, families, business partners, and fellow church members are all around us every day. When it appears after a genuine effort to resolve the conflict that there is no way forward for all involved, do not give up hope. It has been my ability to place these unsolvable issues in this little magic box of forgiveness that has given me the ability to love when it is beyond my normal power to do so, to see the good in someone when part of me does not want to even look, and to be able to rid myself of the horrible weight and conflict associated with these types of issues.

You can HighFive Your Life if you take any of those biting, hurtful, and impossible situations that have weighed heavily on you and move them into the magic box of forgiveness. Just place them there with the caveat that it is not necessary to ever understand them, and that in fact this is okay—that your life is good and that you do not need to understand the "non-understandables." Place them there, and then try to appreciate the value of the soul of the other person. You should not spend your life trying to solve unsolvable problems. The toll on you is not only unnecessary but it is wrong. Move on. Be free. Move on.

HighFive Your Life Principle

Don't beat yourself up trying to understand everything regarding a hurtful and painful situation between people. It is not necessary. Do your best, and then forgive what you do not understand and move on to enjoy your life.

Chapter 40

The Best Four Letter Word

After all is said and done, more is said than done.

—Anonymous

My father and mother are renowned in their community for their ability to work. Everybody just knows that about them. *Work* is the best four letter word I know . . . well, I think *love* and *hope* and *pizza* are pretty good four letter words, too! This book about finding peace of mind by living your life according to the principles in which you believe would not be complete without telling at least part of their story.

Mom—Iris Hilda Dossey—was born in Plant City, Florida, on February 2, 1928. Her family were farmers and so she grew up learning how to make the land produce to feed and sustain their lives. She and her two sisters, Gwen and Lois, are still the matriarchs of our extended family.

Sisters Iris, Gwen, and Lois

They all learned to work on the farm. There wasn't much of a choice. Mom tells the story of hoeing strawberry rows to get the weeds out as a young girl. She accidentally cut off a strawberry bush; then another. Her father told her that if she could not get it right that she would have to go to the house. Soon little Iris was walking slowly to the house, head hung low. He taught her that it was a privilege to work, and that when given a task, it needed to be done correctly. Below is picture of Mom in the strawberry fields that reminds us of this principle.

Work

"If I cut too many strawberry plants while hoeing, daddy would send me to the house... He taught me that work is a privilege."

Iris Larson (Mom) 1928 - Present

Mom attended Florida State College for Women, which became Florida State University by her graduation date. She did not have indoor plumbing at home until she was in college. An outhouse was all there was, and it just had to make do.

Dad—Robert Leon Larson—was born in Illinois but lived most of his life in Sonoma, California. There he grew up working with his mom and dad in their bait and tackle store/bar business. They were active in their community, and to this day there is still a Larson Park in Sonoma named after my grandfather Oscar Larson. Dad went to junior college and then graduated from Stanford.

They met during the Korean War when both were serving in Kentucky at Fort Campbell. Dad was working in the rehabilitation area with those that had lost limbs or had other serious injuries in the war, and Mom was working with the Red Cross. They were an unlikely pair, but love made up the differences.

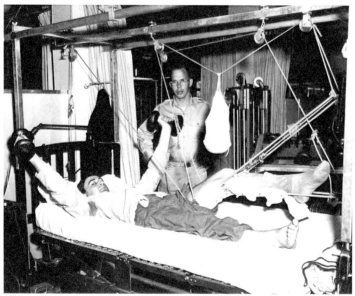

Dad with unidentified patient

Once married and out of the service, they moved to Sonoma where Mom agreed to live for five years, after which time they would move back to Florida. I am sure that Dad was hoping that she would change her mind before the five years were up. My sister and I were born in Sonoma, and Mom and Dad worked in his family's business. It was an interesting combination of a bar and a bait-and-tackle shop. Mom learned how to be a connoisseur of fine Sonoma wines, which was something to say for such a country girl. Things were going well, but the five-year deadline was coming up and a decision had to be made. Would they grow his family's business or move to Florida and start over?

Mom at Fort Campbell

They finally decided that they did not want to raise their kids as owners of a chain of bars, so they decided to move to Florida. It was a very tough decision, and dad's family was not very happy about it. In one of her less wise moments, Dad's mother warned him that if he went to Florida he would fail. Also, while the whole decision to move was being made, his dad was diagnosed with terminal colon cancer.

Up to this point I think Dad had a pretty good life going in Sonoma. He was married, close to his family, playing on the softball teams, active in the community and secure in the family business. I do not think, however, that if Dad had stayed in Sonoma he would have developed the reputation for work that he did in Kissimmee.

Dad and Mom arrived in Florida and decided to settle in a little town called Kissimmee. Their plan was simple: build a duplex and develop a small rental income stream to sustain them while they started over. They brought some money with them and so they bought a piece of property and we lived in a shack that I can still remember. They decided that Dad would not take a job but would instead try and start his own business, whatever that might be. Mom took a job as a social worker to help make ends meet. Dad knocked on doors and tried to get odd jobs such as trimming trees or painting a fence to earn a buck. He built a duplex but then was unable to rent one side so we moved in.

Dad with my sister Danette and me in the early 1960s.

Mom and Dad were motivated by a mixture of the excitement of being totally on their own and the fear of failure. Now that he was in Florida, he was totally isolated, excited yet scared. They went through all of their savings that they brought with them to Florida. I remember reading a letter from Dad to his mother wherein he basically said that he had decided to stop trying to work with his mind and to start working with his back. He asked if he could borrow $5000 to keep things going. That must have been a very hard letter to write. She sent the money to him.

At some point they came across an old broken-down excavating machine, which they bought. Dad was not a mechanic, but he hired one and they were able to get it running. He soon picked up a few odd jobs, and the tide turned in their favor. Working in the dirt or agricultural business was not what Dad had in mind when he moved from California, but he did not care anymore. If it required him to work in the sun and dirt in order to achieve financial success, he and Mom were all for it.

He became acquainted with other people in the agricultural industry, and at some point realized that there was a need for the tile drainage business. This need was found mainly in the vast orange groves all over Central Florida. The government had extended subsidies to these farmers to drain their groves due to the high water table. Dad bought a trencher and that changed the course of their financial lives for years to come.

One of Dad's trenching machines

He found that if he could lay a certain number of feet of pipe in a day he could make $1000. There were really only two things that stood in their way. First was making the sale. Mom told me there were times when he would need to go speak with a grove owner to try and get work, and he would drive back and forth on that lonely backwoods road trying to get the guts to pull into that grove owner's long driveway. I think the fear of not working, however, was much more significant and so he would eventually make the trip to the farm house to ask for work.

The second thing keeping them from success was simply the hard work involved. There was machinery with which Dad was not familiar; machines that broke down; machines that needed parts and that needed them right now to keep the job and crew working. It was not unusual for Mom to gather the kids and go to the airport to pick up a part and drive it to the job. The location of the job was often several hours away from his shop, so early morning starts and arriving home late covered in grease and dirt were the norm. The hot Florida sun and humid climate were almost adversarial. Afternoon lightning storms, mud, muck, and flies were also part of the picture. It was a job that not many men wanted to do. Mom did the books and ran the office out of the home until they could afford to build a shop.

Little by little, however, Mom and Dad began to make money. Dad was no longer interested in anything but work. He worked all the time including Saturdays. Dad worked me and my brother and sister and any friend of ours that happened to come by the house at the wrong time. My high school friends just knew him as Robert L and they knew what it was like to work for him; not much money, a lot of overtime, a lot of dirt, but an uncanny way to teach the importance of work in a competitive free market system. If my college friends came to Florida for spring break, most likely before they went to the beach, they got a good day working in the fields with Dad. He did not believe in headaches. He did not take excuses.

Later in life when he dressed a little nicer, he still drove a low key work vehicle. If he drove up to a job, and saw a bunch of men standing around looking at a busted water line trying to figure out how to fix it as the mud puddle got deeper and deeper, he would just wade right in, nice shoes and pants and all. Pretty soon everyone would be wet and muddy and the pipe would be fixed. That was just his way. It was not his way when he arrived from California. It became his way after he worked with the fear of failure at his heels and the vision to see how to get things done. Both became part of his life.

With the cash flow improving, over the next 25 years Mom and Dad got back into real estate, built two hotels near Disney World, a water park, a pipe manufacturing plant, and became extensively involved in the community. As it turns out, Mom became the best hotel manager that Central Florida has ever seen. She used her wise country business savvy and commanding humility to lead a staff for many years at both hotels. Her motto was "An Atmosphere of Concerned Courtesy," and it showed. Those guests knew they were somewhere special when they stayed at her hotels.

Larson's Lodge and Water Mania located in Kissimmee, Florida

I have always admired her positive outlook on life and her entrepreneurial attitude regarding opportunities. She became a mother figure to many people in our community as she gave freely of her time and resources to those around her. Dad set up an endowment in her name at FSU and each year in Florida at the Governor's Conference on Tourism, the Iris D. Larson awards are presented. These awards were created "to recognize hospitality/tourism industry professionals and students who exemplify the qualities of selfless spirit of service and leadership in their work experience."

Dad passed away in 2005 after an extended battle with Alzheimer's disease (A.D.). It was only an illness that actually destroyed his mind that could keep him down. He had previously battled with prostate cancer, glaucoma, and macular degeneration. Still, he continued with a full head of steam. But when A.D. hit, his will to drive forward was taken from him. It was a tough time for all of us, but especially for Mom. She handled it, however, like the true partner that she was, even when he no longer knew who she was. In 2002, in a moment that nobody could have forecast in the early 1960s when they first got started in Florida, Dad and Mom were both inducted into the Florida Tourism Hall of Fame by then Governor Jeb Bush. What a journey!

You can HighFive Your Life by working. Whether it is fear or excitement or fun or desire to make money or to just make a difference that drives you, work with passion. Don't doubt yourself or your purpose, but if you do start to get shaky, work is almost always the best answer to get you back to where you need to be. It is one of the best four letter words ever created.

My mother Iris Larson with Governor Jeb Bush

HighFive Your Life Principle

Work is the most common and best answer to most common problems.

CHAPTER 41

A Little Here, A Little There

There are no big problems, there are just a lot of little problems.
—Henry Ford

I worked on Dad's pipe installation crews most of my childhood and teen years as time allowed. Dad always gave me more responsibility than would be normal. He taught me to solve problems, work hard, and get the job done. One summer when I was home from college, he sent me to Oviedo to lay drainage pipe in a field where the owner wanted to plant onions. He gave me one crew member who could operate the bulldozer and told me to get the rest of my team from my friends, which I did.

The first day on the job, my father went through the scope of what we needed to do and how to do it. We were required to set up grade stakes so that the big trencher could dig the trench on a slope downhill. The water, once it seeped into the drain pipe, would run downhill to a huge canal that ran alongside the field. Dad was there for a couple of hours giving me instructions and then left. Just like that I was in charge.

We were hardly started when I discovered that my bulldozer operator had driven the bulldozer down a steep bank of the canal so that he could put water in the radiator. He got stuck and could not back up the steep slope. I went over to take a look and did whatever I could think of to get the dozer out. The pipe laying job came to a complete stop as everybody focused on solving this problem. I knew that the property manager had a small dozer so with some embarrassment, I found him and he agreed to bring it to see if we could pull ours out of the canal.

I also began furiously to dig away at the top of the canal bank with a shovel to try and improve the situation. It had no effect but at least I felt like I was doing something. The dozer arrived and did not budge it. The owner called a friend who had an equipment place up the road and pretty soon there was this huge pulling machine with an air-conditioned cab and eight big tires coming our way. We were out in the country with a two lane country road going by the field. People, I suppose other farmers, began to stop on the side of the road and come over to offer their suggestions. I mostly kept digging.

The pulling machine hooked up and did not budge our bulldozer. To my surprise they called for another pulling machine just like the first and it soon arrived on the property. Now we had three machines trying to pull our dozer up the steep bank of that deep canal. We got our big breakthrough when somebody devised a plan for the three machines to work together. The owner's dozer was placed between the two pulling machines. One of those machines would pull our dozer a bit sideways and then the owner's dozer would pull it back straight. Then we would repeat the process on the other side. Each time we did that we would pick up a few inches. We wiggled the dozer up the side of that steep bank a little here and a little there until we got it out. What a team effort! By lunchtime on my first morning of work, unexpectedly I had several hundred thousand dollars worth of new equipment, a bunch of agricultural people offering advice, and a scared and embarrassed crew foreman (me) on my job. It was incredible. There was no charge, no bill for all of the equipment that was used, just the goodwill of hardworking people helping out someone in need. I will forever be grateful for the way they reached out to help me.

There are several HighFive Your Life principles to learn from this story. The one that I would like to share is that often we try and attack huge problems all at once. We give it our all and basically try to dig our way through it, like me with the shovel. Sometimes these problems require solutions that are arrived at "a little here, a little there." Sometimes we need the advice of good people who have our best interest at heart. Sometimes we need outside help to chip away at the problem. You can

HighFive Your Life by recognizing that big problems sometimes need smaller solutions to get your dozer out of the ditch.

HighFive Your Life Principle

Work on your big problems a little at a time. Chip away at the problem while continually seeking solutions.

CHAPTER 42

Did I Really Just Leave
My Three-Year-Old in Detroit?

Blessed is the influence of one true, loving human soul on another.
—George Eliot

I married a beautiful Milwaukee girl and from time to time we go visit her family. Over the years, I have fallen in love with Wisconsin and have appreciated their passion for the Packers, cheese curds, and hunting.

On one such trip, our return flight took us through Detroit, where we had a short 30-minute layover. I was traveling with my wife, Joey, who was pregnant with our third child, our one-year-old, Cal, our three-year-old, Robbie, and Joey's brother, Andy. As you can imagine, our stress level was pretty high. In my opinion, to travel with two infants and a pregnant wife you need at least both grandmothers and a babysitter with you, as well as a variety of sedation type drugs!

As we were preparing for landing, Cal threw up all over the seat. That is when I learned an interesting fact about airline maintenance. When we landed, the airline maintenance crew just came in and replaced the whole seat cushion, which I thought was a great idea. While we were dealing with that, Andy volunteered to take Robbie off the plane for a few minutes, which I thought was another great idea. We (meaning my wife, Joey) were changing the diapers on Cal when we felt the plane start to push backwards. Even in my pea brain, I knew that was a problem. We hailed the flight attendant and let her know that Andy and Robbie had not returned. The plane stopped and soon she returned and said that they were making announcements in the lobby area, but could not find them. She said that they could easily put them on the next flight that left in an hour.

My wife was beside herself, but I convinced her that Andy was a responsible man and it would be okay, so we agreed to let the plane go. By the time we reached the runway a few minutes later, Joey was about ready to have a baby or a cow or something unpleasant. I called the attendant again and told her that we just could not do this. She said that they had located them, that all was well, and they would be on the next flight. With 100-plus passengers ready to go and a plane already on the tarmac, we really did not have an option to return. I once again assured Joey that it would be okay. We took off and had a nervous flight to Orlando. We waited anxiously and, as any good story turns out, they arrived without incident an hour or so later.

Some eighteen years later, after my son Robbie had served a church mission in England for two years and was now in college, we found ourselves once again on a flight together out of Detroit. I was not expecting the emotions that followed as I suddenly reflected on our Detroit experience when he was just three years old. Here he was now, a grown man, sitting next to me. He had been out of country for almost two years. I found myself grateful to all of those who had looked after him when Joey and I were not there: from Andy in Detroit many years earlier to all of his teachers, coaches, and other people that had influenced his life for good.

You can HighFive Your Life by recognizing those around you that inevitably are a good influence on the lives of those you care about, and who take care of you and yours when you are not in a position to do so.

They are everywhere around you, but you need to make sure that your loved ones cross paths with those that will provide this great influence. In addition to family, it could be a great coach or teacher at school. Maybe it is a war veteran or a youth minister at church. People who provide a good influence are everywhere, but it is a choice that you have to make to get them in close proximity to your loved ones.

HighFive Your Life Principle

Recognize and appreciate those around you that inevitably influence the lives of those you care about for good, and who take care of you and yours when you are not in a position to do so.

CHAPTER 43

Get It off Your Chest

Grief walks upon the heels of pleasure; married in haste, we repent at leisure.
—William Congreve

When you do something wrong, you generally feel bad about it. Sometimes a simple apology to correct the situation will do. Sometimes it requires a little more effort on your part to make things right. At our water park, Water Mania, we had many experiences with theft. Our food, inner tubes, gift items, maintenance items and money were constantly under attack from somebody trying to steal them. Sometimes the thieves were caught and sometimes they weren't.

I will always appreciate the letters that I received from two different guests that had done something wrong at the park but wanted to make it right.

> Dear Water Mania, 2/9/99
>
> I am very ashamed of my self. Last spring when I visited you, I cheated you out of about $6 when I claimed my 10 yr old was a child.
> It just caught me!? I had 3 10 & 11 yr olds with me and had budget close. I was very irate that your cut off age was 9 instead of 12 as I had expected. No excuses: Here's the $6 & my apology.
> Sincerely,
> Penitent mom

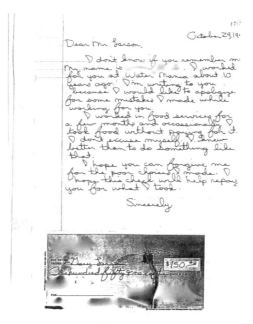

You can HighFive Your Life by unloading the unnecessary baggage of your imperfections. Return what was taken in a foolish moment, apologize for those unkind words, write a letter of explanation and ask for forgiveness, and try to right the wrongs that have been weighing on you.

At the core of Christian thought is the concept of mercy. Mercy cannot rob justice, meaning if a wrong has been done, somebody has to pay the price. We should do our best to pay that price, and after we have done all we can do, Jesus in his mercy will shoulder our sins and atone for them.

A silly but clear example of mercy and justice working together occurred when I was probably five or six years old. Get ready. This is the PG part of this book! I had been playing outside in the dirt road and for some reason which I cannot remember, my older sister by two years had seen my rear end. Someone must have yanked my pants down or something like that. I came crying and complaining to my mother who was cooking at the kitchen stove. I told her that Danette needed to show me her rear end because she had seen mine! Mom hardly missed a beat. She pulled the back of her pants down ever so slightly showing off the top of her right cheek for just a quick second and just kept right on cooking. I was stunned and left completely without words. Mercy had been given to Danette, and Mom had satisfied the laws of justice as I had seen a rear end. Wow. . . . that is forever embossed in my mind, and there was nothing left to say. The dispute was over.

As you experience somebody extending mercy to you when you know you have been wrong, it will make you be more merciful and tolerant in your dealings with your fellow man. Keep your life moving. If you are bogged down by mistakes you have made, do your very best to take care of them and keep moving.

HighFive Your Life Principle

Unload the excess emotional baggage you are carrying by both asking for forgiveness and extending it when and where needed. To the degree possible, right the outstanding wrongs you have done and get on with your life.

Chapter 44

Come Back to Me, Dad

Pray as though everything depended on God. Work as though everything depended on you.

—*St. Augustine*

As I have already mentioned, my father passed away after suffering from Alzheimer's disease (A.D.) for many years. He was pretty much non-responsive in the latter part his life. A.D. is a horrible disease. When you consider the part that your memory plays as it relates to who you are and what and who is important to you, it becomes easy to see why it places a terrible toll on not only the patient but the surrounding family. My mother was amazing during that time.

On one visit, I sat talking to Dad and as usual he was non-responsive. For some reason, I found myself on that day starting to plead with him to come back. After all, he was Robert Larson and could solve any problem known to man. I wanted him to just fix his head and return to us. I began to describe how and why we needed him and began to get emotional; soon I was crying and continued begging him to come back to us.

Then a miracle happened. I looked up at him and he was crying. I couldn't believe it. I do not know if there is a scientific or medical reason for his tears, but I felt like I had broken through whatever fog or stupor that controlled his brain. It did not last long, but it did happen. I had my dad for a brief moment. I had connected and I felt a great sense of love and peace.

I love prayer. It seems like a subject that is somewhat taboo to discuss in our society, though I think a lot of people in this country pray often. Since this is not meant to be a forum for religious discussion, let me just mention that sometimes my prayers may not be very sincere and heartfelt, and perhaps sometimes become repetitive and rote. From my experience with my own father and the focus that I had that day when I tried to bring him back, I know what it means now to really attach meaning to a prayer. Sometimes we need to approach our Maker in humble but intense prayer to connect. I think you will HighFive Your Life when you do.

HighFive Your Life Principle

Intense and meaningful prayer is a good thing.

CHAPTER 45

Do the Undone . . . Sing the Unsung

I have spent my days stringing and unstringing my instrument, while the song I came to sing remains unsung.

—*Tagore*

Have you ever been out with your friends and shared great ideas about new gadgets or creative thoughts for a new movie or book, only to see later that someone else has already done it. Most of us talk a good talk, but very few of us actually take the next step after having a great idea. I have found that by and large, most great ideas seem to be the easy part. It is the execution of the idea where somebody begins to separate themselves from the pack. In this day of instant information flow, you can search the internet very quickly to see if your fabulous idea has already hit the market or if it is still nestled safely in your secret of secrets. If you take the time to actually look, you are way ahead of the rest of the world that for some reason stays in the realm of ideas, never giving what it takes to make the idea a reality. The second step is the most important step—the one where you actually start to do something about your idea.

On one family vacation on the southwest coast of Florida, Mom was worried about having dinner ready when we arrived after a three hour drive. To solve her problem, she decided to put the turkey under the car hood for the ride over. Sure enough it was cooked by the time we got there. That in and of itself separates her from the "normal" moms, but then she went one step further. Being the entrepreneur that she is, she did a patent search to see if the idea was something that she could take to market. It turned out that there was already something on the books, so she left it alone. The point is that she took the next step. You can HighFive Your Life by taking your ideas and doing something with them. You can do the undone.

You can also HighFive Your Life by developing your talents that are untapped. The value of these talents does not necessarily have to be determined by the response or reception offered by others, but should include the joy that it brings to you. Let's take my musical life (or lack thereof) as an example.

My sweet parents made me take six years of accordion lessons as a young boy, including playing "Silent Night" in the local Christmas Parade on a float. It was a hard part of my childhood. I hated practicing for thirty minutes, and it was the source of a lot of contention when I was young. I think it was sports that finally saved me from having to practice, but I guess I should be grateful. Forty years later at our family gathering for Christmas, I am still invited to play the one song I still know, "Silent Night."

In college one of my roommates was a very accomplished guitar player and vocalist. As I watched him play and sing, I began to get this desire to learn the guitar. I bought a very cheap guitar and he would give me a lesson every now and then. It is amazing how much I enjoyed practicing the guitar 1200 miles away from my parents and without anyone else telling me to do it. I loved playing the guitar. Desire is a very powerful tool.

By the time I was a senior in college, my friend had taken me to New York City to buy the acoustic guitar of my dreams at that time. I was getting pretty good and had also begun to sing a little better. As I entered into my mid-twenties it was not uncommon for me to come home from work and plug in the electric Stratocaster and play along with some of my favorite songs. I was never really accomplished but good enough to enjoy the music.

At some point, anyone with a guitar has to write a song. It just seems impossible not to do it. After playing for several years, I had enough songs that I thought I should record them (sometimes it is hard to distinguish between stupidity and doing the undone, singing the unsung). My logic at that time seemed to make sense. It was a sort of reverse logic that went something like this. When I learned how to play a popular song and howled at the moon in the privacy of my living room, I knew how I made that popular song on the radio sound coming from my guitar and my voice. I then made an association that said this sort of sounds like the original song and it's not half bad. Therefore, if I play my own song that I wrote and it sounds half bad, maybe if someone really good sang my song I would have a hit on my hands. Yes, that is what I actually thought.

I decided that I would record my songs and see if I could get someone famous to sing them. Once again, it is the next step that is the most important. I made some phone calls until I found somebody that agreed to speak with me regarding my project. We met and hit it off, and struck a deal. I knew I needed help with the singing, so I invited a beautiful friend and vocalist to sing some of my songs to give it at least a chance of sounding good. We recorded for a week or so and what an experience for me. She sounded great! There I was in a studio with mikes and drums and soundboards and other electronics, along with professionals who made my songs sounds as good as possible. We had several thousand copies of the cassette made and now, thirty years later, I still have several thousand copies of that cassette still available.

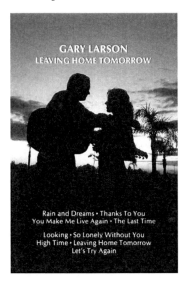

Undaunted, a year later, I reassembled the group and produced another cassette. Besides my Mom and a few people with wax in their ears, nobody much cared for my songs. Everybody on that tape was really good. . . . .the reality was that the songs were just not that good. However, it was an experience that I would not trade.

It turns out that my talent may not be in the writing and performing but in the doing of the undone, in the singing of the unsung. All around us there are people with real talents who would amaze us except they lack the talent of doing the undone or singing the unsung. It all starts not with the first step, but with the second. We are all together on the first step doing what we do, sharing ideas and our voices and our other talents with each other over a burger and soda—and then one day somebody takes the second step and leaves the pack. Everyone blinks for a moment and wonders what in the heck that person thinks they are doing, all the time wishing that they were taking the same second step. If they continue to move forward in a steady fashion with a mixture of patience and persistence, they will ultimately take home a victory for themselves, even if their talent or idea is unappreciated by the masses. Doing the undone and singing the unsung is a victory in and of itself. Nobody's approval is required. HighFive Your Life! Go for it!

HighFive Your Life Principle

If you have a talent, develop it. If you don't have a talent, you're mistaken. You have many. Find them and develop them. Go for it. Do something that seems beyond you.

CHAPTER 46

A Final Thought

I hope that you have been able to relate to some of the thoughts and stories that I have shared. Surely they are filtered through the lens of my life, but I believe that there will be many that will seem familiar to you. I believe this because there is nothing new in this book. I have simply discussed age-old principles that your parents, grandparents, coaches, teachers, and others have taught you. I hope that this book has encouraged you to look for principles being played out in your own everyday life.

Your unique experiences and the principles you have learned from them should be shared with others. As you do this, your sensitivity to the many incredible things going on in your life will increase. You will want to give yourself a high five. You will want to HighFive Your Life.

Thank you for indulging me. I feel like the world needs to hear that the worth of a soul is great, and that we can find peace of mind in this life, even when everything does not go our way. The stories of our lives are among the richest treasures we have. Discover the embedded principles therein, and watch as the silver lining in your life's trials becomes gold.

HighFive Your Life

Read Gary's blog and share your comments and stories at www.highfiveyourlife.com

---